Pop, Rock and Ethnic Music in School

Edited by
GRAHAM VULLIAMY
Department of Education, University of York

and ED LEE
Senior Lecturer, Garnett College, London

CAMBRIDGE UNIVERSITY PRESS
Cambridge
London   New York   New Rochelle
Melbourne   Sydney

Published by the Press Syndicate of the University of Cambridge
The Pitt Building, Trumpington Street, Cambridge CB2 1RP
32 East 57th Street, New York, NY 10022, USA
296 Beaconsfield Parade, Middle Park, Melbourne 3206, Australia

© Cambridge University Press 1982

First published 1982

Printed in Great Britain at the University Press, Cambridge

Library of Congress catalogue card number: 81–9967

British Library cataloguing in publication data
Pop, rock and ethnic music in school.
– (Resources of music)
1. Music, Popular (Songs, etc.) – Instruction and study
I. Vulliamy, Graham   II. Lee, Ed
III. Series
780'.7'2   MT6
ISBN 0 521 23341 0 hard covers
ISBN 0 521 29927 6 paperback

Acknowledgements

Thanks are due to the following for permission to use extracts from material in their copyright:
'Brown Girl in the Ring' by Farian and Klinkhammer (pp. 8-17), FAR Musik Verlag/ Hansa Productions Ltd; 'Mull of Kintyre' (p. 18) by McCartney, MPL Communications Ltd; 'Ring my Bell' (pp. 26-35) copyright 1979 Two Knights Music. Island Music Ltd for the world excluding U.S.A. and Canada; 'Sunday Girl' (pp. 28-35) © 1978 by Rare Blue Music Inc/Monster Island Music Inc reproduced by permission of EMI Music Publishing Ltd; 'Hot Stuff' (pp 28-35) by G. Moroder, H. Faltermeyer, K. Forsey © 1979 by Edition Intro Gebr Meisel OHG Berlin/Revelation Music Switzerland. For the world administered by Heath Levy Music Co. Limited for the U.K. and Eire; Anita Ward 'Ring my Bell and Quantum Jump 'The Lone Ranger', Chrysalis Music Limited; 'Rat Trap' by Bob Geldorf (pp. 19, 20) Zomba Management Publishers Ltd; 'Dreams' by Nix, 'You make loving fun' by McVie, 'Don't Stop' by Nix and McVie (pp 47-9) from *Rumours* and 'Hotel California' (p 229) by D. Felder, G. Freyard and D. Hentey, Warner Bros Music; 1977 Holland Park School Mode 3 CSE syllabus and Examination (pp 58, 59 67-70) London Regional Examining Board; *Harmony at the Keyboard* (p 80) by Reginald Hunt, Oxford University Press; 'With a little help from my friends' (pp 84, 86) from *The Beatles Complete* Music Sales Ltd; 'California Dreamin'' (p 87) by Michelle Gillian and John Phillips, Leeds Music Ltd; 'Hey Jude' (p 122) and 'All you need is love' (p 124) Lennon and McCartney © 1968 Northern Songs Limited for the world.

Cover photograph by Keith Hawkins.

Photographs on p 200 by Neil Sorrell, on pp 176-9 by Roy Gunn.

Contents

Notes on contributors

George Adie teaches part-time at Goldsmiths' College, University of London and in several ILEA schools.

Michael Burnett is head of the music department at Southlands College, London.

Felix Cobbson, Dip. ed. NDD; ATD. (Lon.) lectures in African music. He is the founder of Aklowa (centre for traditional African drumming and dancing), Bishop's Stortford.

John Comer was head of music at Thornes House School, Wakefield. He now teaches music at Greengates School, Mexico City.

Elspeth Compton is the ILEA guitar adviser.

Paul Crawford, after teaching in comprehensive schools, helped set up the Basement Youth Club Music Workshop.

Felix Cross is a professional rock guitarist who has taught both in ILEA schools and at Goldsmiths' College, University of London.

Paul Farmer is deputy head of Dick Sheppard School, London.

George Fisher has taught in London, Leicester and Coventry and has established steel band music in several schools. At present he is a research fellow at Brunel University.

Leela Floyd taught in a large multi-racial comprehensive school in Brent, and is now a freelance writer on music education.

Stewart Knight, after teaching in comprehensive schools, helped set up the Basement Youth Club Music Workshop.

Ed Lee is senior lecturer in English at Garnett College, London.

Neil Sorrell lectures in ethnomusicology in the music department at the University of York.

Piers Spencer lectures in the teaching of music in the Department of Education at the University of Cardiff.

Graham Vulliamy lectures in sociology in the Department of Education at the University of York.

Introduction

GRAHAM VULLIAMY and ED LEE

The aim of this book is to follow up the work done in *Pop Music in School*. In particular, we have set out on the one hand to present a range of practical work, and on the other to point out what seem to us to be the central theoretical issues and the most significant next stages in the development of work outside the more orthodox school music curriculum.

We have been especially concerned to 'build bridges'. To take just one of many examples, Leela Floyd's work on Indian music does not need any great knowledge of Indian music or culture, though we would hope that teachers and pupils might be inspired to obtain such knowledge. Her projects can be performed on simple classroom instruments and will link closely with other approaches to creative work.

Practical work

Part One, along with much of this book, is taken up with projects which have been tried in the classroom by teachers of second- and third-year secondary-school pupils, though the work is often suited to both older and younger pupils. The projects are, above all, practical, cheap and, for the most part, feasible with large classes. The teacher does not normally need much previous training in the appropriate musical style.

A further extension of pop work is that of Paul Farmer and John Comer, who have set out to produce examinable courses. Since traditional music examinations are often felt to be restricting in their content and approach, these teachers (and many others) have sought to incorporate pop within a CSE Mode 3 structure. However, there are dangers in such work which need to be recognised. In order to obtain the possibility of Grade I passes (as an equivalent to an O level) the knowledge and musical approach of popular musicians has to be formulated in terms more acceptable to the academic system. This can result in a distortion of the nature of popular music because of the imposition of inappropriate musical concepts and terminology derived from the totally different ('classical') tradition of music. Another danger is that of overemphasis on learning (and testing) facts *about* music, rather than on participation in musical activity itself. Nevertheless, there is little doubt that, given our present stress on examinations in schools, the advantages of courses like those developed by Farmer and Comer far outweigh these disadvantages. The courses have been exciting and successful for teachers and pupils alike; they demonstrate that the study of pop music can be as serious and thorough as that of any other field; finally, they show that, through working for examinations, it is possible to make the study of pop acceptable to pupils, parents and authorities who might otherwise have serious reservations about such work.

'Sound technique'

The second part of the book, 'Aspects of technique', is in many respects as practical as the work described in Part One. But there is a more fundamental underlying purpose. This is to begin to tackle head-on some of the problems which have emerged as a result of the sometimes over hasty introduction of Afro-American music, and which are troubling both 'classical' and 'pop' aligned musicians.

From the 'classical' point of view, for example, much teaching of pop, rock and folk guitar is seen as inculcating 'poor technique' and 'bad habits'. Ed Lee's chapter on the guitar sought to find the opinions on this matter of three experienced teachers of very different orientation. We were pleased to find that in important respects the differences were more apparent than real, and that, at least in the earlier stages, it is possible to introduce pupils to music in such a way that, however great their interest in popular music, they are not in later years barred access to a broader range of music by restrictive technical habits.

On the other hand, we would not wish it to go unrecorded that the practising rock musicians expressed profound reservations about the imposition of notions of 'correctness', which in fact destroyed any 'feel' or conviction in the player's performance. As George Adie put it: 'Perhaps we *should* teach every pupil as though they were destined for the concert platform, as is sometimes suggested. But the question is, *which* concert platform? It is too easily assumed that this must mean the classical, rather than the folk, jazz or rock concert platform.'

We thus return to a recurrent theme throughout our work, namely that different musics are related to different contexts and need to be evaluated using different criteria. This being so, it is presumptuous to assume that the music with which one is most familiar is necessarily 'the best' or that its techniques are of universal application. There is not one definition of 'good technique', but many.

Our belief that this is so meant we had to make several difficult choices because of limitations of space. For example, in preparing Chapter 6 we worked from the conviction that the electric guitar is an instrument whose techniques are complex enough to merit a description at least as detailed as that normally given to the first steps in classical technique. But our first criterion for selection had to be whether a project would be suitable for the largest group of pupils – beginners or those with a low level of skill. Furthermore, we sought to include projects which would link easily with other, and more orthodox, approaches. As none of the teachers felt that it was essential to *begin* on an electric instrument it seemed best to deal with the subject on another occasion when there is space to do so.

Ethnic musical styles

Our attitude to music leads inevitably to the adoption of a cross-cultural approach. A more detailed exposition of our view of the value of and indeed of the need for a multi-ethnic approach to music is to be found in our Preface to Part Three and in the chapter 'Alternative criteria' in Vulliamy and Lee (1982).

In several important respects, popular music styles have more in common with diverse non-Western musics than they do with the 'classical' music of our own society. Like non-Western musics generally, Afro-American music, the major influence on contemporary styles of popular music, is conceived and mediated in an oral-aural fashion. In contrast to this, even though there is always scope for interpretation, 'classical' music is defined through a notated score. As a result, there are very strict limits outside which deviation from the score is not permissible. Consequently our traditional conception of music tends to have been limited to those aspects of the sound experience that can be accurately notated. The details of this argument are spelled out in Wishart (1977) and in Greene (1972). The argument is not, of course, that composers such as Bach could only compose through the medium of notation, since Bach probably improvised far more chorale preludes than he ever wrote down. The point is that *what* he improvised was significantly and indeed crucially shaped by the prior existence of a particular notational system. However, in the case of popular and ethnic music, this notation system is of little importance, or is completely absent. Thus both popular and ethnic musics share certain common characteristics, which are not generally incorporated in the 'classical' tradition. Examples of these include the use of radically different timbral qualities elicited both from instruments and from the human voice, and the consistent use of microtonal variations of pitch. Therefore a positive feature of incorporating both pop and ethnic music into school teaching is that it serves to enhance pupils' understanding of how sound has been explored and structured by musicians, as well as leading to a more sympathetic and less ethnocentric view of music generally.

Teacher-training and research

Two final important points have emerged from our work on this text. They are not likely to be welcome at a time of economic stringency, but we feel that the need to face such realities should not prevent us from pointing out the directions which we believe should be taken when it becomes possible to do so.

Firstly, every step which we take in developing work in this vast field makes even clearer the severe limitations of the pre-service and in-service training of teachers in this respect. The fact that we have felt it necessary to include, for example, the chapter by John Comer on rock and blues piano styles, which is in some ways so elementary, is just one indication of this deficiency. Again, it is noteworthy that the three guitar teachers of radically different interests and backgrounds, who were interviewed for Chapter 6, make a similar point: music teachers continue to be trained in establishments which consider nothing but 'serious' music. Students keen to learn about jazz or rock find few teachers in such colleges who either know anything about Afro-American music or have mastered even the most basic skills in this musical tradition (such as improvising on a twelve-bar blues sequence).

A positive alternative was indicated during a visit to Sweden by one of the editors in 1978. A new experimental music teacher training college, Sämus, in Malmö, has been so successful that the government has taken its approach as a blueprint for all music teacher training colleges in Sweden. *All* the music students at Sämus learn about a wide variety of music and how to perform it – classical, avant-garde, folk, jazz, blues, rock and so on. *All* the students, in addition to their main instrument, learn to play guitar, piano *and* a drum set – such flexibility proving an enormous asset to the future school music teacher. It is significant that Stewart Knight points out that some mastery of these skills is essential if one is to undertake this type of work. Careful attention is paid to those practical skills necessary for future classroom teachers who intend to use a wide variety of music in their teaching. Thus, in addition to the traditional skills taught to prospective music teachers, emphasis is placed on (amongst other things) piano and guitar accompaniment, blues improvisation, tablature notation for guitarists, a basic knowledge of the electronic apparatus to be found in rock groups, and a knowledge of different drum styles. With such training, music teachers can no longer remain ignorant of the type of music with which their pupils are most familiar. But, in the absence of such training programmes at the moment, it becomes even more important that ventures such as the Basement Youth Club Music Workshop, to which we devote Part Four of this book, should be actively encouraged in all our large cities. There, school pupils have the opportunity to be taught by teachers with a specialist knowledge of rock styles, using facilities best suited to this idiom.

Our final point concerns the near total lack of research into fields other than 'classical' musicology (with the honourable exception of ethnomusicological studies of non-Western musics). We will cite here an analogy from language work: if a teacher is to teach well, he or she needs materials, and such materials have to be built upon accurate descriptions of language (notably grammar) and of language acquisition. And yet, to move back to the musical sphere, what research has been done shows the total inapplicability of transplanting both the notation system and terminology of classical music to varieties of popular music (see Shepherd *et al.*, 1977). Elsewhere, the editors have charted the beginnings of a 'grammar' and aesthetics of popular music (Vulliamy and Lee, 1976, 1980, and Section Two of Vulliamy and Lee, 1982). But the fullest encouragement should now be given at higher degree level to more detailed analyses of this type. This will then enable the kind of work which we have advocated in this book to be based on a solid foundation.

References

Greene, G. K., 'From mistress to master: the origins of polyphonic music as a visible language', in *Visible Language*, Vol. 6 (1972).

Shepherd, J., Virden, P., Vulliamy, G. and Wishart, T., *Whose Music? A Sociology of Musical Languages* (Latimer, 1977; Transaction Books, 1980).

Vulliamy, G. and Lee, E. (eds.), *Pop Music in School* (Cambridge University Press, 1976; 2nd edn 1980).

Vulliamy, G. and Lee, E., 'The aesthetics of popular music', side 2 of *Popular Music* (tape plus booklet) (Sussex Tapes, 1979).

Vulliamy, G. and Lee, E., *Popular Music: A Teacher's Guide* (Routledge and Kegan Paul, 1982).

Wishart, T., 'Musical writing, musical speaking', in Shepherd *et al.* (1977; 1980).

PART ONE   CLASSROOM WORK

Editors' preface

This section of the book aims to give accounts of projects which both enhance ana-lytical listening and relate directly to performance and creativity. Such a stress resists the temptation to substitute learning *about* pop for learning *about* classical music. Here we would heartily concur with a conclusion from one of the few pieces of structured research into the effectiveness of using pop music in school music lessons: 'knowledge of the musical idiom through active participation in perform-ance, listening sessions and discussion is more valuable than mere *facts* about the songs or performers' (Sarah, 1976, p. 162). All the projects in this section can be per-formed with simple, standard equipment and materials, and they are designed for and have been tested with large classes.

The contributions of John Comer and Michael Burnett overlap to some degree, though the latter focusses particularly on work with younger pupils. Nevertheless, these chapters provide a fund of materials and will usefully illustrate the different results obtained by teachers with somewhat different philosophies of music and approaches to pop. The important thing, we believe, is that they both demonstrate the immediate applicability of a more traditional training to much 'charts' pop music of mass appeal.

Paul Farmer's and John Comer's approaches to the examination of pop music may also be compared. Both demonstrate that pop music is a serious study which can not only be incorporated into orthodox curricula, but can also serve as a useful area of comparison to standard classical works. In addition, Paul Farmer's work is shown to be highly relevant to the involvement of 'less able' pupils who would nor-mally have no hope of taking examination courses in music.

A minor point about the organisation of this book should be made here. The part of Chapter 7 by Piers Spencer, entitled 'Vocal improvisation' (pp. 117–26), might also have been included in this first section, since it describes practical classroom projects. However, we felt it was desirable to keep it together with the other work on pop singing included in Part Two.

References

Sarah, P. J., 'School music and the adolescent' (unpublished M. Phil. thesis, Univer-sity of London, 1976).
Vulliamy, G. and Lee, E. (eds.), *Pop Music in School* (Cambridge University Press, 1976; 2nd edn 1980).

1 How can I use the Top Ten?

JOHN COMER

In this chapter my aim is to present ways in which pop can be used in general class teaching with 13- to 14-year-olds in comprehensive schools. For most pupils this is the last year in which they will have a compulsory music lesson. They will almost certainly only have one lesson a week and, in some schools, my own included, even less than that. Pop – and that includes current hit singles – gives teachers a tremendous opportunity to make class music into a practical, listening and interpreting activity which stems directly from what the pupils are familiar with and enjoy.

The approach to pop I am suggesting here is divided into *structured listening*, which is designed to reveal the component features of pop, and the *reproduction* of some of these features in the classroom. The aim is to lay the basis for the pupils' understanding of musical elements through aural perception and to confirm their knowledge through practical activity. Many of the concepts and activities are pitched at an elementary level. I am not assuming that pupils know anything about music as 'a subject' or that they can play any instruments. The range of ability and interest varies considerably from set to set and even among pupils in the same set. I do assume, though, that some pupils will be encouraged to take up music in the fourth and fifth years, which will give them the advantage of more intensive work in smaller groups and where they will be able to follow a more individualised curriculum, perhaps within the framework of a Mode 3 CSE course.

As accounts such as that of Rogers (Vulliamy and Lee 1976; 1980) show, it is a mistake to see 'pop' as a homogeneous form. Nevertheless, it can be helpful for immediate purposes to see the whole field of Afro-American music and its derivatives as sharing common characteristics: the use of chord sequences, regular verse forms, highly emphasised percussion, syncopation, improvisation, riffs and ostinato patterns, and a wide range of vocal styles. Teachers will find, however, that though it is a sound first step to present the music in these terms, exceptions will regularly be found in current hits. From the teacher's point of view it is also important to remember that pop is predominantly music for use, and especially for dancing, although in some areas great importance is attached to attentive listening and to the lyrics. It is also a music based on electronic technology, giving it unique timbres and an enormous dynamic range.

However, pop is not just a musical style, but a manifestation of a set of meanings, a shorthand reference to larger personal and social values. It would be wrong to deal with it simply as 'classroom material' providing an alternative route to more traditional goals of music theory. The meanings of pop are not only embodied in musical sounds; they are as much contained in the lyrics, the style of singing and the genre (punk, soul, reggae, disco, rock'n'roll) and are closely linked with new dances, fashion and self-presentation through such publications as *Smash Hits*, *My Guy*, *Disco Fan*, *Mates* and *Fab*.

When selecting material for use in class, it is as necessary to choose carefully from the pop repertoire as it is from the classical. Tracks from a progressive rock album are as likely to be inappropriate for a class of 13-year-olds as is *The Art of Fugue*. Even within the body of the Top Ten there are many records which, for a variety of reasons, don't lend themselves to class use. I am going to concentrate on three singles, which have had particular value for me. These should satisfactorily illustrate my point that pop can provide suitable material for the teacher who wishes to make aural demands on his pupils, and who wishes to involve them in practical activities.

All three songs can be approached in the following ways:

(1) *The melody*. Singing, playing on instruments.
(2) *Rhythm work*. Clapping rhythms of a piece, notating rhythms, reproducing rhythms on instruments. Percussion work.
(3) *Harmonic awareness*. What are chords? What are chord sequences? Representing sequences on paper. Reproducing them on instruments.
(4) *Verse forms*. The structure of songs.
(5) *Lyrics and Meanings*. Writing out lyrics from the record. Comparison of lyrics. Writing lyrics to a chord sequence.
(6) *Style and instrumentation*. Functions of the instruments. Features of the pop style. Comparison of styles. Technical aspects of sound production.

'Brown Girl in the Ring' by Boney M, which headed the charts in the spring of 1979, has a bright, catchy tune which is straightforward to sing; the lyrics are repetitive and easy to learn by heart; the harmony is extremely basic – two chords only. Like other traditional folk songs it is well weathered and accessible and yet it has

Example 1

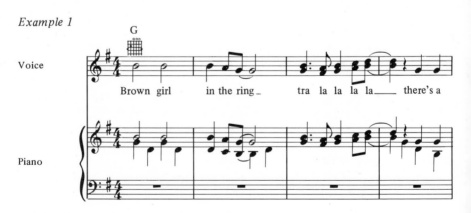

the excitement of a modern arrangement by a glamorous black group. Example 1 gives the chorus with which it opens.

The simplicity of the harmonic scheme, which it shares with many Top Ten songs, makes it an ideal introduction to chords and chord sequences. Two chords are easy to remember for a beginner guitarist or pianist or a pupil playing a bass-guitar part; attention can quickly be directed from the physical articulation of the chords towards using the chords to make music. Making music, in this context means playing chords in sequences; playing chord sequences in co-ordination with others, using notation or from memory; differentiating the functions of rhythm, harmony and melody through the use of different types of instrument; relating melodies to harmony; becoming aware of how music is organised through the use of sections and repetition; and collectively performing songs.

My experience is that pupils have great difficulty in 'hearing' harmonic changes. There is also little awareness that chords in popular music are organised in sequences. Asking a class of 13-year-olds to 'write down' the chord sequence of the chorus of 'Brown Girl in the Ring' is to ask the impossible without very careful preparation of the most basic musical elements – What is a beat? What is a bar? What is a chord? What is a chord change? What is a sequence? How many chords are there in this sequence? These are some of the ways I have prepared pupils for listening to 'Brown Girl in the Ring' and to other popular music.

When working on chords and chord sequences, one should start straight away with pupils themselves playing through simple sequences on the guitar or the piano. Prepared guitars – guitars tuned to a specific set of related chords (see Appendix for details of tunings) – are an invaluable means of enabling pupils without training to participate in group music making. Under the teacher's guidance pupils can reproduce the chord structure of a song simply by strumming their instruments at the right time, and subsequently accompanying the class in singing. The teacher should have a conventionally tuned guitar to direct and reinforce what the pupils are doing, although the piano can be used as an alternative. The classroom piano can also be used to provide the bass notes of chords or an elementary bass riff. Before playing through a sequence let the performers get an even strum, four crotchets to a bar, just throwing the chords back and forth to experience the point of change where one stops and the other starts. More problems are likely to arise from timing than from knowledge of the sequence. Pupils often spontaneously speed up, as they do in percussion work; if they do, make sure that they do it evenly and on the teacher's signal return with a proper *rallentando* to the original tempo. Once pupils have got used to strumming they should learn to play four- and eight-bar sequences such as those in Example 2.

Let each chord last one bar, but vary the time signature and the rhythms that are used. More than anything it is the rhythmic movement of chords which causes the initial problems in hearing the underlying progression (especially when, in a syncopated style, chords are tied across the bar line) and so some practice here is important. A few basic rhythms for pupils to use are suggested in Example 3. Children have a great imitative capability and can easily play rhythms demonstrated by the teacher that they could not read from notation though, of course, there is no reason why rhythmic notation should not be taught as well.

Example 2

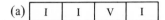

(a) | I | I | V | I

(b) | I | I | ♭VII | I

(c) | I | V | V | I

(d) | I | II | V | I

(e) | I | IV | V | I

(f) | I | IV | I | V

(g) | I | IV | I | V/I

Example 3

(b)

    I   V   V   I

(a)

    I   I   V   I

(c) *

    I   II   V7   I

(d)

    I   IV   I   V

(e)

    I   IV   V   I

* The sign ( ) above this and subsequent examples indicates that, following jazz convention, when a piece to be interpreted with a 'swing feel' uses rhythmic figures which are notated as ♩♪ (or ♪♪), they are actually to be performed as something nearer to .

These sequences can as easily be used by the teacher for purposes of chord recognition. In this connection I would like to make a general point about methods of enabling pupils to represent aural experience. I have found it extremely important that pupils should first prepare a space in their books, draw boxes or grids, or number the side of a page, so that they have a clear format in which to represent their knowledge or perception; many pupils have appeared to fail simply because they did not know how to write down what I asked of them. Let me take the question of how pupils represent a short chord sequence. If they are to listen to four bars of music I would ask each of them to write out the following grid beforehand:

1 2 3 4	1 2 3 4	1 2 3 4	1 2 3 4

This establishes a very specific context in which to write down what they hear, which may, for example, be the sequence:

I	I	V	I

Initially, pupils can label chords using letters as in Example 4. Identifying common chords and the dominant seventh is the basic preparation for a study of harmonic progressions and there is a lot of scope in this preparatory work for discovering which progressions are more pleasing than others. Does the progression

I	I	I	V7

sound right? Why does it sound right if it is followed by this progression?

V7	V7	V7	I

Four-bar patterns can quickly be extended to eight bars once these initial exercises are understood.

Longer sequences can be built up by repetition or by linking sequences together. In both listening to them and playing them pupils build up a sense of 'the bar' and of four-bar phrases. In listening to the teacher playing a sixteen-bar section they should learn to identify four-bar sections within it. Better still, the teacher can write down some sixteen-bar sequences on cards and make use of a number of pupils to play the sequences through while their classmates write them down. Example 4 shows a typical result.

A consistent, regular performance of a chord sequence by a group of pupils is, to

Example 4

Pupil's score

A	A	B	A
A	A	B	A
A	C	A	B
A	A	B	A

Actual chords

I	I	V7	I
I	I	V7	I
I	IV	I	V7
I	I	V7	I

my mind, the proof that they understand what a chord sequence is: for instance, it is only when pupils have successfully *played* the three bass notes of a twelve-bar blues in the correct order, with others playing the chords, that they show the delight of genuinely understanding the principles involved. I can think of many occasions when this has happened.

Pupils are not generally aware that songs are organised into verses, choruses, introductions, codas, instrumental breaks or bridge sections and need to have these terms clearly explained. Can any of the pupils write down the order in which the various sections occur in 'Brown Girl in the Ring'? Are the verse and the chorus the same length? They should be given a chance to hear the record again and to notate its structure, for instance by writing down the initial words of appropriate lines – 'Brown girl', 'Old head' – and by indicating other musical activity (eg 'Instrumental'). They can later tabulate the result using 'verse' and 'chorus', or letters for the various sections. The result is an elementary formal analysis which is made in the process of sorting the song out for performance. The result in a pupil's notebook might look something like the grid in Example 5.

The chord sequence of the chorus and verse of 'Brown Girl in the Ring' should also be established by carefully directed listening. How many bars long is the chorus? Count out with the pupils like this: *1* 2 3 4 / *2* 2 3 4 / *3* 2 3 4 / *4* 2 3 4 / etc. Without a system like this many pupils who could easily perform the task will become

Example 5

Brown girl	A
Show me	B
Old head Old head	C
I remember I remember	D
Brown girl	A
Show me	B
Old head Old head	C
I remember I remember	D
Brown girl	A
Instrumental	E
Old head Old head	C
Brown girl	A

confused. (To avoid the complications of split common time I halve the number of bars and describe it as being in $\frac{4}{4}$ time, the minims becoming crotchets.) The chorus and the verse should again be presented as a grid but this time in conjunction with the lyrics. With a prepared grid such as Example 6 and with preliminary practice along the lines suggested many pupils should be able to write in the chords and the changes where they occur.

Example 6

(A)	(A)	(B)	(B)
Brown girl in the ring	tra la la la la___	Brown girl in the ring	tra la la la la
(A)	(A)	(A/B)	(A)
Brown girl in the ring	tra la la la la___	She looks like a sugar in the	plum, plum plum

(A)	(B)	(B)	(A)
Old head water run	-'dry	nowhere to wash my	clothes.

Although I want pupils to be able to hear and write down what they hear (and play what they hear), if classes do have difficulty in representing harmonic changes there is always the possibility of taking a more playful approach. I have had groups at one table stand up when they hear a chord change and sit down again when it changes back. This is often surprisingly effective in the sense that, after one or two verses, groups get the hang of it and one can see them getting ready to stand up, that is, anticipating the chord change, at the right time. It is important, for all my emphasis on writing and the value of symbolic understanding, to acknowledge that not all pupils are equally adept or prepared for it and alternative ways of showing understanding should be kept in mind. Obviously, performance on an instrument is an ultimate in this respect.

Playing these sequences through using plain crotchets confirms the regularity of the chord changes, but it is not difficult for the guitarists to progress to using a more rhythmic accompaniment:

If there are two guitars for each of the two chords the accompaniment can take on even more rhythmic and percussive life by splitting the two functions, so that the first guitar might play even crotchets, with the second guitar playing accented quavers on the second and fourth beats of the bar:

If the department can afford guitar slings, encourage the pupils to hold their instruments in the correct manner for a pop instrument. They learn from the outset to strum up and down in front of the body and the left hand is free to damp the strings. Pupils playing the quavers in the illustration above would need to damp the strings to play their part accurately. Plectrums give a better volume and a more penetrating tone.

Piers Spencer has covered many aspects of improvisation in his chapter, 'The blues: a practical project for the classroom' (Vulliamy and Lee, 1976; 1980, p. 74). Pentatonic improvisation makes it possible to work with the same five notes to some extent, regardless of whether the underlying chord is I, IV or V, but in a non-blues style the primacy of the triads must be respected. The improviser must know which notes belong with which chords and change these sets of notes when the chord changes, just as the melody does. Some pupils may be familiar with pitched percussion instruments and be able to play the melody along with the accompanying instruments. Other pupils can be introduced to melody playing in a very simple manner through the use of riffs (repeated melodic phrases), where the knowledge required is barely more than that of the basic sequence. The players should be familiar with the melody and be shown how it is based on the two triads. If this is done with the whole class, the melody can be written down with the chord underneath it on a separate stave, with the passing notes put in brackets:

Example 7

There are many things to explain here – sharps, tied notes, dotted notes, apart from the more elementary facts of the stave, the clef and note names. Even so, it is visually clear that the melody notes and the chord notes are the same. The triads can be practised by the melody players at a crotchet pulse but as soon as possible they should move on to an ostinato pattern such as the one below, based on the root note of each chord, and preferably derived from the song itself:

Example 8

This rhythmic pattern can be kept while other notes of the triad are introduced:

Example 9

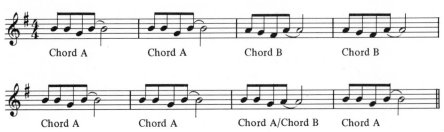

Passing notes can be introduced in a similar manner, gradually incorporating variations:

Example 10

Simplified versions of the brass riffs actually used on the record give greater authenticity to what the pupils are doing and, further, demonstrate what riffs are and that they are being used at all. Many pupils are not consciously aware of instrumentation except in striking instances. A teacher who can play a reed instrument can give a strong lead in introducing these riffs. The kazoo fits well with the sound and with practice some exciting colour can be added to the performance, for example:

(simplified brass riffs)

Chord A   Chord B

With 'Brown Girl in the Ring' I have concentrated on the use of chords and harmony with the ultimate aim of bringing together instrumentalists to play and to accompany the class in performing a song. In a class of 25–30 I use four on percussion, four on guitars, two on piano/bass guitar, one or two playing riffs and a group or the rest of the class singing. The performance should be staged, with 'the band' in an appropriate place in the room. Having the use of two microphones in recent months has extended the sense of doing it 'for real'. A final point I would like to make is the great value of tape recording the result. The tape recorder is so much more than just a means of playback. Operating the recorder and microphones and working to realise a good sound balance is an activity in itself which some pupils are particularly keen on. Getting a good sound on tape is certain to mean a number of different takes and each take gives the performers more practice. Students realise more what goes into making a record, the kind of discipline, care and plain repetitive work that needs to be done. Finally, I think that making a recording is a help in bringing about higher standards of performance. If performers don't start together or trail off at the end unsatisfactorily it is there for all to hear, and the teacher can insist that the result is at least good enough to satisfy commonly agreed standards. Although there are schools with synthesisers and high-quality recording equipment, most of us will probably have to do what we can with a less-than-perfect mono recorder. But it is still well worth bringing it out into the centre on occasions.

'Mull of Kintyre' by Wings was top of the hit parade for several weeks in the autumn of 1977. Everything I have written about 'Brown Girl in the Ring' could have been written about this song and for more or less the same reasons: there are a limited number of chords (I, IV and V), a slow rate of chord change and the chords fit into an easily graspable pattern. The chord sequence and the organisation into verse and chorus can be arrived at by the pupils in a similar way. It is in $\frac{3}{4}$ time with a typical folk-style accompaniment – the root of the chord picked out on the first beat of the bar and beats 2 and 3 strummed. Pupils have no difficulty in imitating this. Although the melody is pentatonic, it is strongly linked to the chord structure and any improvisation or riff making should take this into account.

Though the lyrics of many pop songs can appear so trivial and cliché-ridden on the printed page, they can still be sung expressively and communicate feeling. The lyrics of 'Mull of Kintyre' are a model of conventional nostalgia. The singer has 'travelled far' and 'seen much' but his thoughts are always returning to home. The production of the record includes a band of highlanders playing pipes, adding an original touch to the sense of a world of strongly held values and commitments. It is precisely because they are such a 'model' that they are useful in stimulating pupils to write lyrics in a similar vein. With any currently popular song it is valuable to find out first how much the pupils already know about it. How many pupils know the words of the chorus? Can they write them down in their books? Does anyone know all the words by heart? Playing the record as a reminder is already part of the programme of structured listening that means that the pupils are not just listening to the record but listening *for* something. Even with well-known songs there are always surprises, discrepancies between what the pupil had always thought the words to be and what they actually are.

The word setting of 'Mull of Kintyre' is very straightforward. The syllables fall exactly on the beat or on the quaver spaces in between (Example 11).

Example 11

Mull	of	Kin -	tyre		Oh	mist	roll - ing		in from	the
	2	3		2	3		2	3	2	3

sea	My	des -	ire		is	al - ways	to		be	here	Oh
	2	3		2	3		2	3		2	3

Mull	of	Kin -	tyre_____				
	2	3		2	3	2	3	2	3

Pupils should copy an outline scheme such as Example 11 into their books to make sure that their versions do fit the number of beats and, moreover, that they fit their lines to take account of the chord changes. Emphasise that they are imitating a style and that the closer they approximate to it the better. I have witnessed many pupils distinctly impressed that their own pastiche of a verse of 'Mull of Kintyre' is every bit as good as the original. A few of these can be selected and sung to a chordal accompaniment. It is not usually the easiest occasion to keep a straight face!

As I said earlier, pupils are not generally aware of production techniques in popular music, and particularly of arrangement and instrumentation. A method I have used to introduce this (apart from formal work on 'How a record is made') is to give pupils a list of instruments and musical effects to find out which ones they can hear being used on particular records. One that I have used for 'Mull of Kintyre' is: electric guitar, electric bass, acoustic guitar, electric organ, piano, male vocals, female vocals, two-part singing, chorus, brass, saxophone, bagpipes, bass drum, snare drum, tom-tom, cymbal, tambourine. The list is educative in itself in that it suggests a range of possibilties even when they are not all being used. But, more importantly, it sets up the requirement for every pupil to listen and discriminate. Faced with a choice between 'electric guitar' and 'acoustic guitar' the pupil cannot simply write 'guitar' or, faced with named percussion instruments, simply write 'drum'. The list should also be used to draw attention to questions of arrangement. Which instrument was playing at the beginning? At what point do the bagpipes come in? Do the bagpipes stop playing after they have played the chorus or do they play more quietly in the background? When the class comes to perform this song themselves an 'arrangement' should be worked out in advance, some players coming in at agreed times for special effects.

The world of 'Mull of Kintyre' and the world of 'Rat Trap', a song by the Boomtown Rats which also reached Number 1 in the Hit Parade (autumn 1978), could hardly be further apart. Punk rock represents a white, working class frustration with society. It is an aggressive style musically, with a powerful emphasis on ostinato patterns, parallel harmonies, a fast beat, a shouted vocal style and some of the most original lyrics (along with reggae) to come out of the pop scene. Pupils I have talked to about punk say that 'Punk tells the truth' and that 'Sham 69 are telling it like it is'. They have a clear idea that many Top Ten songs are simply expressing trite and meaningless sentiments by comparison. 'Rat Trap' epitomises the protest side of this music and I have used it with many groups to explore the meaning of songs and what groups are trying to express. Interest in the words of hit songs is very much on the increase as they have widened in range and meaningfulness. Nearly all the teeny-bopper magazines I referred to in the introduction print words of current songs and some (*Smash Hits*, for example) exist entirely for that purpose.

It is clear that pupils often get the gist of a song but are not bothered whether they hear every word correctly and it is important to set up the situation where they have to listen actively. By far the most productive approach I have found for getting pupils to listen is to duplicate an outline of the lyrics and ask them to write in the remaining lines and half-lines while the record is played. Below is given the outline that I have arrived at for 'Rat Trap'. A few pupils will be able to complete this (the first verse and the middle section) in three hearings, depending on their prior knowledge of the song; many more will be able to do so on a further hearing.

RAT TRAP   THE BOOMTOWN RATS

1   There was a lot of rocking going on that night
2   Cruising time . . .
3   . . .
4   The five lamp boys were coming on strong
5   . . .
6   The pulse of the corner boys . . .
7   . . .
8   . . .

1   . . .
2   He says the traps have been sprung before he was born

```
 3   He says 'Hope bites the dust . . .
 4   And pus and grime ooze from its scab-crusted sores
 5
 6
 7   But you can make it if you want to . . .
 8   You're young and . . .
 9   Anyway it's Saturday night, time to see what's going down
10   Put on the bright suit Billy . . .
11   It's only 8 'o clock . . .
12   You don't know what it is . . .
13   You'd better find a way out, hey . . .
14   . . .

 1   In this town Billy says, '. . .
 2   In this town Billy says, '. . .
 3   Hey you walk
 4   Switch from your left to your right
 5   You push in . . .
 6   It tells you . . .
 7   Billy take a walk/take a walk . . . with me.
```

All the class have something concrete to do and a comprehensible format in which to write in what they hear. Classes are genuinely eager to complete their scripts (on Banda sheets) and press to hear the song again even after four hearings. Although the task might seem mechanical – just a matter of writing in the words – in fact I have found it to have an extraordinary diagnostic potential. The song is sung at a fast tempo and to complete the script successfully requires high concentration, aural acuity, quickness and accuracy of judgement. It is clear at a glance which pupils show these qualities. It is not a 'culture-free' test: most of the best scripts I have had have come from bright working-class girls and boys who know and like the song. A duplicated sheet of lyrics actually sung should be given at the end for pupils to compare with their own and subsequently the whole song should be played through. The value of this approach is the thoroughness with which pupils come to know the details of a song. (I have done similar types of work in studying folk music and the effects of aural transmission. I have given pupils a duplicated sheet of lyrics on which they have had to mark all the modifications which are present in a performed version of the song. For example, when we compared Louis Killen's version of 'The Blackleg Miner' with that of Steeleye Span we found at least a dozen minor modifications: words sung in a different order, words omitted altogether, different words used. Again, it requires a high degree of concentration to get good results. Pupils are also hearing fine songs, having to think about the meanings of the words and, not least of all, each individual in the class is actively involved.)

The work on 'Rat Trap' continues with questioning and discussion, after which pupils write a paragraph expressing what they think the Boomtown Rats are trying to say. I have often used 'Rat Trap' in conjunction with other songs of a similar type, comparing lyrics and styles, and occasionally in conjunction with Pink Floyd's

song 'Money' (from *Dark Side of the Moon*) which presents the very opposite side
of life, the world of opulence and greed and which also sets up the opportunity to
compare different styles of music within the pop/rock orbit. Here is an example of
detailed and thoughtful work by a girl in an upper set.

The song 'Rat Trap' shows the life in a low-down city without any money or anywhere to go. Billy is a young lad experiencing life in the suburbs with all the violence
and crime. He has no money, nowhere to go on a night and, evidently, no friends.
His sister Judy evidently has pretty much the same problem only she can't do anything at home because of her's and Billy's parents always fighting. She just walks
around and when she digs 'down in her pocket and finds 50p' she decides she will
get herself a good job with plenty of money.
    Billy is also fed up. Everyone tells him he must obey the law and stick to rules.
Everybody's telling him what to do. The city is noisy and dirty and full of crime.
He goes to the Italian cafe and gets drunk because he is so fed up with life. He wants
to get out of town but he knows it would never work out for him. So he is stuck in
the town for the rest of his life without a job and it depresses him. His sister is also
in the same position but she has the willpower to try and get a good job and earn
some money. (Amanda Lewis)

The best of pop music lasts. Most of my pupils are familiar with fairly recent
successes – Ralph McTell's 'Streets of London' (1974) or Steeleye Span's 'All
Around My Hat' (1975) – but also with the Beatles, 'When I'm 64' (1968) and
further back still, Elvis Presley's 'Jailhouse Rock' (1958). A number of songs come
back again for a second or third hearing. Child have recently issued the seventh version of 'Only You' (1956) and we may yet have a punk version of 'Blue Moon',
already more than twenty years old before Elvis Presley sang his version in the
1950s. There is a tradition of popular music here to be uncovered and used by
teachers, both as music history and as songs for performing.
    I have restricted this chapter to work I have done with full-sized classes of third-
form pupils. Work of this type will be valuable with other age groups, but with older
groups the range and depth of work using popular music can be considerably
extended. Drawing up a Mode 3 CSE course for fourth- and fifth-year groups, allow-
ing for an equal balance of popular and classical music to be studied as set works
and building into the syllabus the composition, arrangement and performance of
popular songs, has transformed my working experience with those groups. For
details of this syllabus see p. 70.
    The greater attention given to practical work has enabled some pupils to make
great advances in their ability to perform. The willingness of two especially keen
guitarists to hump their guitars and amplifiers to school and back twice a week or
more confirms beyond doubt my belief that pupils want to attain an authentic
sound and that to use pop in school demands authentic instrumentation: an amplifier with several inputs, electric guitars, an electric bass, two microphones with
stands and a full drum kit as a minimum. Even a gesture in this direction can be
effective. I have fitted my guitar with a transducer, a small pick-up which attaches

to the body of the instrument, and it can be played through an amplifier or through the auxiliary input sockets of the department record player. Even such simple amplification has meant that on many occasions it has been able to substitute for a bass guitar. In the classroom it is impossible to achieve the goal of complete idiomatic authenticity, yet it is a measure of the practical applicability of pop that achieving the proper idiom can be discussed at all. Individual teachers will attach different value to different parts of the programme I have suggested here. But there is no doubt that pop can be used, for a wide range of classroom work as well as extracurricular work, and is no less demanding for educational purposes than any other music.

References

Rogers, D., 'Varieties of pop music: a guided tour'
  and
Spencer, P., 'The blues: a practical project for the classroom'
  both in
Vulliamy, G. and Lee, E. (eds.), *Pop Music in School* (Cambridge University Press, 1976; 2nd edn 1980).

APPENDIX: GUITAR TUNINGS

Example of guitar tunings in the key of E

Standard tuning: *String*: 1   2   3   4   5   6

   Note: E   B   G   D   A   E

Alterations are denoted as follows:

   G ↑ G ♯   means 'Re-tune G string upwards to G sharp'.

	Guitar 1	Guitar 2	Guitar 3	Guitar 4	Guitar 5	Guitar 6
String	Chord I	Chord IV	Chord V	Chord V7	Chord II	Chord VI
1	E	E	E ↓D♯	E ↓ B	E ↓ C♯	E
2	B	B ↑ C♯	B	B ↓ A	B ↓ A	B ↑ C♯
3	G ↑ G♯	G ↑ A	G ↓ F♯	G ↓ F♯	G ↓ F♯	G ↑ G♯
4	D ↑ E	D ↑ E	D ↑ D♯	D ↑ D♯	D ↓ C♯	D ↓ C♯
5	A ↑ B	A	A ↑ B	A ↑ B	A	A ↓ G♯
6	E	E	E ↑ F♯	E ↑ F♯	E ↑ F♯	E
	E major	A major	B major	B7	F♯ minor	C♯ minor

Alternatively, all the guitars can first be tuned to the same chord, and capos can then be used to change some of them to whatever other chords are required. (This will produce parallel harmonies.) In sequences such as I/bVII/bVI this is much the easiest way. Here is an example:

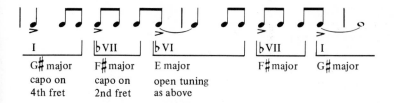

I	bVII	bVI		bVII	I
G♯ major	F♯ major	E major		F♯ major	G♯ major
capo on	capo on	open tuning			
4th fret	2nd fret	as above			

2 Using pop music with middle-school classes

MICHAEL BURNETT

The middle-school years are above all a period of discovery. Facts about the world, about people, about culture, about so many things have been acquired during the pre-school years, and in the primary and junior school. But between the ages of 10 and 13, and beyond, youngsters want to discover more about what they already know; they begin to question facts which before went unquestioned; they begin a voyage of discovery.

This chapter is concerned with the use of pop in the middle-school music curriculum, and its principal aim is to help children to set off on such a voyage of discovery into pop music itself, and so to discover that what they already know and accept in general terms is, like a model train set, something built of a number of basic components which together constitute a whole. These components are common to all pop songs but can be put together in such a variety of ways that each song assumes its own identity; and in examining, playing and experimenting with such components, taken from songs with which they are already familiar, the children can discover in pop a new dimension which can add immeasurably to their pleasure in listening and participation. Even more important, perhaps, this process will enable them to invent components of their own and ultimately to put these together in the form of original compositions. After all, every 12-year-old knows that when an adult sits in the driving seat of a motor-car and performs a number of simple physical operations the car will carry its passengers from one place to another. Yet how much more interesting the journey becomes for the youngster when the driver explains the meaning and purpose behind the operations. Similarly, every middle-school pupil knows that he or she derives great pleasure from the resultant combinations of sounds when certain pop musicians perform together, whether on stage or in the recording studio. Yet how much greater that pleasure can become if the music teacher explains (or, better still, leads pupils to discover) the basic components and their purposeful combination to create that musical experience.

Of course a demonstration of the components of, say, a Beethoven symphony movement could be pleasurable, too, although it is arguable that, with the best of intentions, a young adolescent would emerge from the demonstration with little more than a hazy notion that a symphony movement contains a number of tunes, each of which is played a number of times by different instruments of the orchestra. Hazy or not, this notion is, of course, important in terms of music education since,

if our children are to come to perceive the formal structure of the music of
Beethoven, one has to begin somewhere. And hazy notions can gradually be replaced,
over a period, even if it is some years, by a true understanding of the complex devel-
opmental workings of a symphonic movement. However, young adolescents are not
always willing or able to see the value of enlightenment in the long term: they want
to know *now*, not next year. This being so, there are two fundamental reasons why
pop music can provide enlightenment sooner rather than later about some basic
aspects of musical composition. Firstly, some form of pop music is part of the personal cultural experience of every young adolescent. Secondly, the constituent components of many of the pop songs which 10- to 13-year-olds find most appealing
lend themselves, by their very nature, to demonstration on classroom instruments.

Before going further I'd like to examine those reasons a little more closely. The
pop music which a young adolescent most usually enjoys has a number of characteristics which help distinguish it from the vast spectrum of pop as a whole. (This
spectrum, incidentally, has never contained a greater variety of musical styles than
it has in recent years, when it ranges from the aggressive musical naivety of the Sex
Pistols through the smooth sophistication of Abba to the long-winded introspection
of Pink Floyd.) Generally speaking, the pop most likely to have middle-school
appeal will be found to have an overall simplicity of form if it is described according
to the criteria we would apply to a work of a classical master. The constituent components of a song – rhythmic and harmonic accompaniments, riff patterns, melody,
basic structure – each of these will usually have a simplicity of conception which
immediately suggests the use of classroom instruments for demonstration and recon-
struction. Take, for example, a song which is in straightforward binary form and
employs a simply conceived diatonic or modal melody of limited range, supported
by an accompaniment consisting of beat-based percussion rhythms and harmonically
of perhaps two chords only. Such a song lends itself to performance on classroom
instruments whereas more complex musical styles – pop or classical – render transcription from one medium to another impossible.

At this point I risk the accusation by purists that I deny the essence of pop music
by suggesting that its basic components should be played on xylophones and melodicas, rather than electric and amplified acoustic instruments, where the latter are
not available. And the purists are right essentially. Electricity is fundamental to pop
style and volume an important aspect of it. But I believe that music teachers are
generally people who are in favour of doing something rather than nothing. The
argument that pop music should not be played in the classroom because the school
has no electric instruments or means of amplifying acoustic instruments is con-
vincingly pure but musically sterile.

It is time now to turn from the general to the specific. My intention here is to
give examples of typical pop-song components which are playable in the classroom
and at the same time taken from recent Top Thirty hits. The four songs concerned
each appeared in the British Top Thirty lists during the same three-week period in
June 1979. They are as follows:

Anita Ward	'Ring My Bell'
Blondie	'Sunday Girl'
Donna Summer	'Hot Stuff'
Quantum Jump	'The Lone Ranger'

Form (basic structure)

At an early stage of practical work it would be helpful to introduce your class to simple basic (binary and ternary) song structures. For formal clarity 'Ring My Bell' could hardly be bettered, consisting as it does of the binary pattern: repeated verse (A) – chorus (B). Form is intangible and something which many young adolescents – not to mention adults – find a problem to comprehend, and yet this Anita Ward song has the necessary brevity and clarity of outline to ensure a grasp of the implications of a simple binary form. As in all pop, the chorus is instantly recognisable not only because of the feeling of tension which immediately precedes it but also because it regularly employs the same set of words – in this case, 'You can ring my bell'. Here is the formal outline of the piece. Each section is eight bars long, the introduction and interludes making use of the same chord pattern as the other sections:

Example 1

Intro – duction	A	A	B	B	A	A	B	B	Inter- lude 1	Inter- lude 2	Inter- lude 3	B	B

Blondie's 'Sunday Girl', although sounding rather more musically obvious than 'Ring My Bell', actually uses a slightly more complex form which, although basically binary, depends for its effect on the introduction of a third (C) section which appears once only.

Example 2

length in bars	4	8	8	8	1	8	6	8	8	8	8	8	8	8
	Intro – duction	A	A	B	Inter- lude	A	A	C	A	A	B	B	B	B	B fading

This more sophisticated formal approach is common in those songs which use sequences of major chords as the basis of sections A and B (see p. 28 for an analysis of the chords used in 'Sunday Girl'). Section C provides an opportunity to introduce a minor sequence for contrast and variety.

'The Lone Ranger' is a fascinating example of a basically monothematic song which is given additional interest by the interjection of a subsidiary theme on three occasions. Of course the existence of this second theme does not give the song a binary form. However, it does provide a useful classroom example of another approach to the use of two musical ideas.

Example 3

length in bars	4	24	24	4	4	24	8	8
	chant	A	A	chant	chant	A	A	A

In addition, the imaginative use of imitation Red Indian chanting in the subsidiary section makes the piece a potential stimulus to further experiments with vocally conceived rhythmic patterns.

Rhythms

Rhythmic drive is a fundamental part of pop music. The drummer in a band has the dual role of setting and maintaining a pulse for a particular piece of music and delineating important structural points during the song (for example the beginning of the chorus section) by altering the tone colours and/or rhythmic constituents of what he is playing. But, whereas the pop drummer plays a number of rhythms simultaneously on the various instruments at his disposal, in the classroom it is necessary, and no less effective, to allocate each rhythmic component to a particular pupil and instrument.

For example, in 'Sunday Girl' there are three main rhythms. Rhythm (a) is played on guitar and cymbals, (b) on side drum and (c) on bass drum. For classroom performance I suggest that (a) be allocated to suspended cymbal and wire brush, or tambourine, (b) to medium-pitched drum and (c) to low drum:

Example 4

'Ring My Bell' makes similar use of straightforward crotchet and quaver rhythms, although the bass-drum patterning is in two-bar phrases and a dotted figure is added. Suggested classroom percussion equivalents to the original instrumentation are included in the rhythm chart shown in Example 5.

Example 5

count	①	2	3	4	②	2	3	4
tambourine	♩♪♪♪ ♪♪♪♪				♪♪♪♪ ♪♪♪♪			
medium/ high drum	𝄾	♩	𝄾	♩	𝄾	♩	𝄾	♩
low drum	♩	𝄾	♩	𝄾	♩.	♪ ♩		𝄾

During the chorus section of Donna Summer's 'Hot Stuff' the bass drum plays firmly on the beat throughout, side drum on beats 2 and 4 and the cymbal introduces a more complex, syncopated quaver, crotchet, semiquaver pattern. Classroom alternatives are once again suggested in Example 6.

Example 6

count	1	2	3	4
tambourine or cymbal	♪ ♩	♫♪ ♩		♫
medium/ high drum	𝄾	♩	𝄾	♩
low drum	♩	♩	♩	♩

Chord sequences

Much of pop music's basic simplicity as compared to classical music stems from its modal/diatonic nature. Since the advent of a distinct form of young people's music in the middle 1950s, pop has tended to reject the classically influenced chromatic harmony of popular song of the thirties and forties. This has been largely replaced by a strongly folk-influenced, modal style, with a marked preference for the use of a minor tonic chord (I minor), and the major chord build on the flattened leading note (bVII major). The major scale is used a great deal too, usually diatonically, although occasionally modulation from the tonic major to the relative minor occurs. In the four pop-song examples quoted in this chapter the only form of key-shift which occurs is in Blondie's 'Sunday Girl' where, at bar 29, the entire musical structure is taken up a tone. This practice of shifting everything by a tone or semitone is relatively common in pop – I must admit to finding it crude and usually quite irrelevant – but it is generally not classified as a modulation, a term which refers to a *process* of key change. This apart, 'Sunday Girl' is an example of the use of diatonic major key. Only five chords are used: I, IV and V (major) as the basis of verse (section A) and chorus (section B), with the addition of III and VI (minor) to provide that element of contrast in section C which was mentioned earlier. Example 7 is a chart showing the chord sequence used in section A of 'Sunday Girl'.

Example 7

count	① 2 3 4	② 2 3 4	③ 2 3 4	④ 2 3 4
xylophones	e e g	a a b	c c g	a a b
glockenspiels and/or chime bars.	C C	F G	↓C C	F G

⑤ 2 3 4	⑥ 2 3 4	⑦ 2 3 4	⑧ 2 3 4
c c g	a a b	c c g	c c g
↓C C	F	↓C C	C C

The chart is primarily designed for use with those classroom instruments on which the letter names of notes are indicated (the glockenspiels play the bass-drum rhythm of the original, xylophones are allocated the tambourine rhythm), but any other available instruments may of course join in too.

As a general rule, when using chord charts such as Example 7, pupils should aim to start on the lowest practicable note and subsequently move the shortest distance between adjacent notes. For example, *e* to *g* should be a third, not a tenth, *c* to *d* a second rather than a ninth. Exceptions to this rule are indicated in the charts by the use of arrows which show whether the leap should be up or down. Capital letters are employed to distinguish the root of a basic triad from its other constituent notes.

'The Lone Ranger' is, by way of contrast, purely modal in harmony and, of all the songs which have been mentioned, is the most economical in terms of the number of chords used. In fact the song is based upon two chords only: I (minor) and V (minor), with the modal flattened seventh of the scale forming the minor third of the latter chord, which is used in first inversion. The chart in Example 8 represents the entire chord structure of each 24-bar-long verse of the song:

Example 8

count	① 2 3 4	② 2 3 4
xylophones	D f a f	e a e a
glockenspiels	D D D D	c

(The important bass-guitar tune which supports this chord structure will be examined later under the section dealing with riffs).

'Ring My Bell' uses a four-chord (rather than two-chord) sequence, which is repeated throughout and forms the basis of both verse and chorus sections. The original song is in C minor, a key which clearly makes difficult a direct transcription for classroom instruments. I have accordingly transposed the chord sequence to the more practical key of E minor. (This also makes the sequence accessible to young guitarists, who should play chords of E minor, A minor and B major as indicated.)

Example 9

count	① 2 3 4	② 2 3 4	③ 2 3 4	④ 2 3 4
xylophones	g　b	c　a	g　b	b　b
glockenspiels	E　　E	A　　A	E　　E	B　　B
guitars	Em	Am	Em	B

Donna Summer's 'Hot Stuff' is predominantly in the Aeolian mode, based on the note G. Again, in order to avoid accidentals which are impracticable on classroom instruments, I have transposed the chord sequences to an E-based Aeolian mode. Chord charts for verse and chorus are as in Example 10 (glockenspiels use the original bass-drum rhythm, xylophones the side-drum syncopations).

Example 10

VERSE

count	① 2 3 4	② 2 3 4	③ 2 3 4	④ 2 3 4
xylophones	E　g	b　g	a　a	b　g
glockenspiels	E E E E	E E E E	D D D D	E E E E
guitars	Em	Em	D	Em

CHORUS   ┌─play 3 times in all──────────┐

count	① 2 3 4 ③ 2 3 4 ⑤ 2 3 4	② 2 3 4 ④ 2 3 4 ⑥ 2 3 4	⑦ 2 3 4	⑧ 2 3 4
xylophones	‖: A　d	E　b :‖	A　c	d　B
glockenspiels	‖: A A B B	↓E E E E :‖	A A A A	B B B B
guitars	‖: Am　Bm	Em :‖	Am	Bm

Riffs

A riff is a short melodic phrase which, repeated, forms the basis of an entire pop song, or section of a song. (There is some parallel in classical music in the use of ostinato patterns; however, composers in the two fields differ, both in the way in which they construct music around the ostinato, and in their purpose in doing so.) Pop-music riffs are usually played in the bass and are often modal in flavour, with particular emphasis on tonic, minor third and seventh of the scale. The fact that riffs are usually limited in range makes them particularly suitable for performance on classroom instruments if transposed up by an appropriate interval. Take, for example, those which occur in 'Hot Stuff' as the basis of part of the chorus section and in 'The Lone Ranger' as the fundamental element which supports the entire musical framework. Transposed from G to E modal minor, the riff from 'Hot Stuff' is as follows in Example 11. Note the importance of the initial minor third leap, the riff's limited range and the characteristic use of syncopation:

Example 11

The 'Lone Ranger' riff is more complex rhythmically and melodically, as might be expected in a case where the riff constitutes the most important element of an entire piece of music. As the riff stands it is rather impractical for classroom tuned percussion, because of the use of fast single-note dotted rhythms and the sliding semitone elision f – f♯ – g:

Example 12

However, it would not be difficult to produce a more feasible riff for use in the classroom which preserves the outlines of the original 'Lone Ranger' example:

Example 13

Melodies

Pop melodies tend to be purely modal or diatonic, are most often organised in short four-, six-, or eight-bar sections and, above all, are designed to be easily memorable. These three factors alone facilitate transcription for classroom instruments; when one remembers that many pop songs use a limited range of notes, the idea of adaptation for classroom use becomes even more feasible. Take, for example, the delightful instrumental tune with which 'Hot Stuff' begins. Suitably transposed, and with due allowance made for the fact that the chromatic slide in the original (marked *) is impractical in the context, Example 14 is a melodic fragment which, played on recorders or melodicas, could illuminate in the classroom a musical experience which might otherwise be in danger of being merely passive, a tune heard on the radio and that's all:

Example 14

This experience would, of course, be considerably heightened if, the tune having been learned, a group of pupils were to be selected to play it to an accompaniment provided by a second group and based on the 'Hot Stuff' chord chart (Example 10), with a third group adding the rhythmic components (Example 6).

To take another example, the chorus section from Anita Ward's 'Ring My Bell' suits recorders and melodicas admirably, and its organisation has a clarity which could serve as a useful model for young composers. Again, I have transposed the tune from C minor to the more practical E minor and have included (for 2nd recorder/melodica) the chorus interjections which play such an important part in the original. (Once learned, I suggest that the tune should be accompanied harmonically and rhythmically as indicated in Examples 9 and 5 respectively.)

Example 15

I hope that the teacher will by now be convinced of the practicability of performing pop-song components in the classroom. Of course, transcriptions such as those given above are not possible unless the teacher has a real and positive interest in the music of young people. Indeed, it may well prove necessary for the teacher to learn from the taught in this particular context, a process which can prove beneficial to all concerned. Certainly many teachers would add to their own musical development if they were to use their skills as analysts and arrangers to facilitate the kinds of musical experience outlined above. Moreover, even if the youngsters' voyage of discovery into pop were to end at this point, much of value would have been achieved; in particular there would be a deepening of a young adolescent's appraisal of a vital aspect of his or her cultural life. However, the journey ultimately has a destination which is just as important, that of enabling the pupil to come to terms with his or her own creative potential; for, having seen and experienced in practical terms how pop music is constructed, the pupil is in a position to create music independently along similar lines.

Composing pop songs

The process of composing pop music is essentially an aural one. Pop musicians may use some form of notation once a tune and its harmonies have become defined, but the act of composing is dependent in the first place upon aural trial and error. This method of composing - play first, notate (if necessary) afterwards - clearly has advantages in relation to middle-school work. However, guidance from the teacher is still needed. By providing concrete examples of the sort outlined above, the teacher lays the ground-work for realistic experiment of a kind which I shall illustrate below. Some ability to cope with notation, such as we can reasonably expect from pupils in this age-range, can only be an advantage in setting down successful ideas.

For example, we looked earlier at the basic components of the rhythmic accompaniment to Blondie's 'Sunday Girl' (Example 4). These components are each very simple, and it would not take a great deal of ingenuity on the part of pupils (1) to redistribute the rhythms amongst the instruments already specified (low drum plays the tambourine part and so on) and (2) to experiment with a medium drum part which instead of going | ♩ ♫ ♩ ♩ | became | ♩ ♩ ♩ ♫ |

or | ♩ ♫ ♩ ♫ | .

Subsequently we examined the chord sequences used in the various songs under discussion. Having seen how the verse section of 'Sunday Girl' employs the chord progression (major) | I | IV V | I | (see Example 7), pupils could experiment with alternative versions of the same chords, for example

| I | V IV | I | or | I | IV I | V | .

In the process they could well discover other, just as effective, diatonic chord progressions. (Classroom instruments with letter names of notes indicated are particularly useful here, once the concept of the triad and its use has been established.) For example, 'The Lone Ranger' uses the chords of D minor and A minor as its basis (see Example 8). Why not encourage your pupils to experiment with D minor and E minor (instead of A minor) for a change, or even to move on to the commonly used Dorian pop progression D minor–E minor–F major–E minor? Again 'Ring My Bell' has four chords, in the order E minor–A minor–E minor–B major. What does the progression E minor–B major–E minor–A minor sound like? Or E minor–B major–A minor–E minor? Or why not spread the progression over eight bars, rather than four, by doubling the length of each chord?

Riffs can provide a particularly promising area for experiment largely because of their brevity and modal emphasis. (Again classroom tuned percussion instruments are invaluable for the purposes of playing and creating riffs because of the ease with which modal scales may be demonstrated and comprehended.) Taking, for example, the rhythmic and tonal basis of the riff from 'Hot Stuff' (Example 11) as a starting-point, pupils should be encouraged to try out for themselves alternative note sequences. Example 16 shows merely a few examples of riffs based on the one used in Donna Summer's song. They are tabulated in increasing order of complexity, although they may all be played with ease on tuned percussion. (Once learned, it is desirable for riffs also to be played on any bass instruments which may be available – low on the piano keyboard or on a cello, for example.)

Example 16

The composition of pop melodies is perhaps the most demanding of the creative activities so far mentioned, and thus will require more direct guidance from the teacher. It would be helpful if the broad outline of binary form, with its verse (A) and chorus (B) sections, were revised prior to the pupils beginning their experiments, and it is important that the budding composers think in terms of four-, six- or eight-bar sections when working out their melodies. This need not be too difficult a process as the building up of a tune by the repetition of short melodic fragments is funda-mental to pop and therefore should be encouraged. The pupils will also need guid-ance about the choice of mode or scale, and about how the key note is established by repetition, and by its use at important moments during a tune (beginning and end, for example). The pupils should be led to see that in those cases where a mode or key with a minor inflexion is chosen, the minor third of the mode is often given special emphasis (likewise the minor seventh). Finally it is wise to encourage the youngsters to think in terms of a limited compass (a fifth or, at most, an octave) and to avoid large leaps in their melodies.

The following example of a complete tune may prove helpful as a model. It can be played on recorders, melodicas, or any other melody instruments which are available:

Example 17

Section A

Section B

Once the tune has been learned, it may be accompanied as follows:

Section A   Take the first two chords of 'Ring My Bell' (see Example 9), and repeat as a sequence a total of eight times.
An untuned percussion accompaniment may be provided by repeating the 'Sunday Girl' rhythm pattern (Example 4) sixteen times.

Section B   Take the 'Hot Stuff' riff (Example 11) and repeat eight times. The lowest pitched instruments available should play the riff; it would sound particularly effective if doubled two octaves lower on piano.
A chordal accompaniment may be provided by repeating the first chord of the 'Ring My Bell' sequence a total of 16 times.
For rhythmic accompaniment the 'Hot Stuff' pattern (Example 6) should be played 16 times altogether.
The song may be introduced and/or concluded by repeating any one (or more) of the components a set number of times, and an interlude could be included on the same kind of basis.

The results of the experiments outlined in this chapter will almost certainly not result in a musical equivalent of Donna Summer's 'Hot Stuff'. However, the results will be positive, both because pupils will come to see how pop music is constructed and because they will develop those creative energies which can so easily be neglected during the years of middle-school education. It is to be hoped as well that such positive results will help contribute to the breaking down of those musical barriers which so easily become erected during the early years of adolescence. From such a removal of barriers both teacher and taught can benefit immeasurably, and the voyage of discovery into all that music has to offer will, as a result, be made easier.

References

Details of the records mentioned in this chapter are as follows:
Anita Ward, 'Ring My Bell', TK Records S TKR 7543.
Blondie, 'Sunday Girl', Chrysalis CHS 2320.
Donna Summer, 'Hot Stuff', Pye / Casablanca CAN 151.
Quantum Jump, 'The Lone Ranger', Pye / Electric Records WOT 33.

Further resources

Michael Burnett is the author of the following works which are designed to initiate and support practical work with middle-school pupils.

'Making up a pop song', *Music Stand* (Chester, September 1974).
'Music Stand's Patent Pop Song Kit', *Music Stand* (Chester, September 1976).
These projects include melodies, chord sequences, rhythmic patterns and riffs along the lines suggested in this chapter.

Mr Tambourine Man (Chappell, 1977).
Yellow Submarine (Chappell, 1977).
By the Rivers of Babylon (Chappell, 1980).
These arrangements are from Chappell's *Pop into School* series. Recorders and/or melodicas are essential and there are optional parts for glockenspiels, xylophones and untuned percussion.

Pop Music Topic Book (Oxford University Press, 1980).
This is a survey of the history and musical characteristics of pop from the middle 1950s to 1967, with information on the various styles from 1967 to the present and the links between pop and other forms of music. Each section of the book contains questions and practical projects related to the text. The projects are intended for performance on classroom instruments. Use is made of chord charts similar to those outlined in this chapter.

'Coming to terms with pop', *Music Teacher* (Evans, February to December, 1972).
This is a series of articles which details the history of pop up to 1972 and includes some guidance on practical work in the classroom.

APPENDIX: A POP-SONG KIT

The kit is intended to form the basis of a classroom pop song along the lines explored in this chapter. It contains each of the principal components of a binary-form song: melody, chordal accompaniment (which incorporates a riff) and rhythmic accompaniment. Suggestions are made as to possible instrumentation, but it should be stressed that these suggestions are entirely optional and that other instruments may be used either as additions to those suggested or as replacements for them.

CHORD CHART (incorporates riff)

Section A   play 4 times in all

count	① 2 3 4	② 2 3 4	③ 2 3 4	④ 2 3 4
xylophones	: D f a ↓D	C C C C	D f a ↓D	C C Cd e :
glockenspiels and low piano (riff)	: D D	C C C C	D D	C C Cd e :
guitars	: Dm	C	Dm	C :

Section B   play 12 times in all

count	① 2 3 4	② 2 3 4	1 2 3 4
xylophones and low piano (riff)	: D D f D fG	G f e :	D D
glockenspiels	: f a	G b ↓d :	D D
guitars	: Dm	G :	Dm

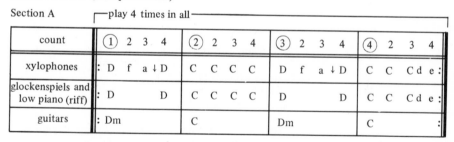

RHYTHM CHART

Section A

Section B

Once each of the components of the kit has been allocated to a group of pupils, practised and learnt by them, the song may be put together in a variety of ways. Here, for example, is a possible one-verse format:

		bar no.	
Introduction		1	low drum begins with section A rhythm
		3	medium drum enters with A rhythm
		5	tambourine enters with A rhythm
		7	xylophones, piano, glockenspiels and guitars enter with A chord sequence
Song	A	11	recorders and/or melodicas enter playing section A
	B	27	all instruments change to section B material
		51	end of section B; recorders and/or melodicas stop
Conclusion		52	all instruments other than melody instruments change to section A material
		56	xylophones, piano, glockenspiels and guitars stop on first beat
		59	untuned percussion stop

Obviously there are many alternative formats. For example, instead of beginning with untuned percussion, the Introduction could start with xylophones and glockenspiels, perhaps playing section **B** material rather than that from **A**, and drums and tambourine could enter later. Instead of only one verse it would be possible to incorporate two verses with an interlude for untuned percussion between the two. Or the interlude could be based on the riff pattern, with xylophones and piano playing their section **B** material while a glockenspiel or recorder extemporises a Dorian mode tune.

3 Rhythm and percussion work in rock and Latin American styles

JOHN COMER

Rock rhythms

Rhythm and percussion work is both musically valuable and of great interest to pupils, because they associate it with the highly rhythmic styles of pop and rock. However, a paradox I have found is that although when the teacher claps a two-bar rhythm pupils are immediately able to clap the rhythm back, nevertheless many of them are unable to maintain a basic beat regularly and have poor rhythmic independence of hands, or hands and feet. Nor can they play accurately from even simple notation. This suggests two fronts on which to approach rhythm and percussion work. On the one hand, basic concepts have to be built up: I assume that teachers will be familiar with courses which set out to develop such skills. On the other hand, it is also important to use the imitative capacities of pupils to go more quickly into practical work of greater variety and complexity, drawing on their familiarity with popular idioms and their enthusiasm for them. My aim in this chapter is to suggest how one might begin to do this.

Pupils listening to pop and rock music hear a battery of percussive effects and have little idea that the kit drummer, for all the nuances and subtlety of the performance, is essentially repeating the same one- or two-bar rhythms over and over again. The drummer is seen as performing a total activity with his body rather than as co-ordinating a number of separate rhythms simultaneously. The approach I take to rhythm and percussion work follows from this. 'Rhythm' can be presented as the repetition of 'rhythms', which are short, regular motifs: these can be heard (on record, with proper preparation), learned in the form of musical notation, memorised and performed. Groups of pupils can play several of these different rhythms simultaneously and thus simulate the sound produced by the kit drummer. It can also be shown how the drummer keeps time not only by counting beats within each bar but, more importantly, by counting the bars and knowing what point has been reached in an eight-, twelve- or sixteen-bar verse form. Pupils can be taught to feel these larger units of time and use them in their percussion work.

Though in the earlier lessons the teacher is unlikely to be introducing the cross-rhythms which are most characteristic of popular music, it is worth bearing in mind that pupils have no more difficulty in imitating syncopated rhythms than on-the-beat rhythms, though they have great difficulty in notating them at this stage.

[40]

In making rhythms, it is not necessary to rely on percussion instruments; finger clicks, slapping the thighs or forearms, foot tapping and vocalisation are all valuable. A number of contemporary pop dances involve sequences of stylised hand and arm movements and may account for why examples such as the following are invariably greeted with such enthusiasm:

1	clap	slap	thigh	clap	clap
2	finger click	slap	thigh	clap	finger click
3	slap right forearm	clap		slap left forearm	slap right forearm

Sitting round in a circle is the best situation for exercises and games of this kind; the teacher can be clearly seen and movements can be made more freely. In a circle it is possible to 'pass claps round the class'. The teacher claps (or slaps etc.) a one-bar phrase which is taken up by the next pupil, who passes it on to the next. After six pupils, say, the teacher introduces another phrase until there are three or four claps passing round the group. If instruments are being used, sitting in a circle also makes it easy to move them round to the next set of pupils so as to let everybody have a turn. Using even simple two-bar phrases steps up the concentration required considerably. To establish a mood of concentration combined with enjoyment I haven't found anything to beat 'O'Grady says', using a mixture of clicks and claps.

With some groups (and this has worked best with upper sets) I have combined rhythmic with vocal imitation, humming motifs built around the pentatonic scale. Here are some examples of the type of phrase used:

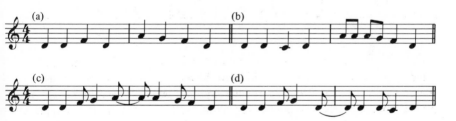

Another valuable approach with these motifs is to play a twelve-bar blues sequence on the guitar as an accompaniment, the teacher and pupils changing to one-bar phrases in bars 9 and 10, and 11 and 12.

These short rhythms are all starting-points for pupils to learn the note names and values, to recognise them aurally and visually, to be able to write them down and clap or play them on an instrument. One value of pupils learning notation is that scores can be designed which consolidate the use of some of the rhythms which have come out of classroom games and practical exercises. Example 1 shows a 'Percussion Sheet' I have used with pupils at this stage:

Example 1

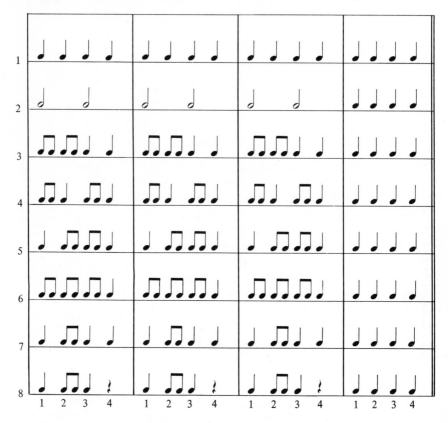

All the pupils are given a copy (duplicated on a Banda sheet) and the free-standing percussion set up in the middle of the room with the sheets on music stands. Pupils can play through particular rhythms; two or more rhythms can be played simultaneously; two pupils can play through the first four, for example, in canon; dynamic gradations can be brought in and the sonorities of the different instruments exploited according to the kind of beater used or the part of the instruments struck. Three or four pupils playing together and keeping good time sound very effective. Even at this stage, when rhythms are not being employed in a pop or rock manner, it adds enormously to the value of the work if the teacher plays through a popular chord sequence on piano or guitar while the pupils play their parts. They have to count, to know where they are in the chord sequence and end exactly on time. The sheet has been designed with a different rhythm in bar four to assist this understanding and also to prepare them for more advanced work where thinking in groups of bars rather than single bars is essential.

I am going to assume in this chapter that the music department has a basic drum kit and one or two Latin American percussion instruments. A minimum outfit would be: a bass drum with foot pedal, a snare drum, a hi-hat cymbal and, in addition, claves, maracas and (ideally) bongos or a tom-tom or a tambour.

The drum kit is the symbol as well as the fact of rock percussion. Pupils immediately recognise rock rhythms played on it, which shows how distinctive and universal those rhythms are and how specific the balance of sonorities is. Here is an example of the basic combination of rhythms used:

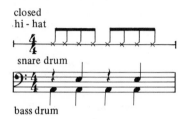

It looks simple in notation (and can quickly be learned) but I have only found a few pupils able to pick it up straightaway or continue it for more than one or two bars. Rhythmic independence of hands and feet is a skill which needs preparation, training and practice to develop. Try asking the pupils how many of them can pat their head and rub their stomach in a circle at the same time. A few are sure to be able to do it. Can they do it reversing their hands? Many pupils have learned this trick – co-ordinated independence of hand movements – but they have only learned to do it one way and are as helpless as the others when asked to reverse their procedure.

By playing these rhythms separately on the drum kit and then bringing in each in turn, the pupils can see and hear that the overall sound is made up of rhythms in combination. Let one of the pupils take over the cymbal part and then another the snare drum. Let groups of three produce the whole sound themselves. With a group that has a confident, steady tempo it enhances the sound considerably to play with them on the piano: it offsets the dryness of purely percussive sound and emphatically relates their playing to the rock idiom. I have often used a blues/rock sequence on the piano in a style like this:

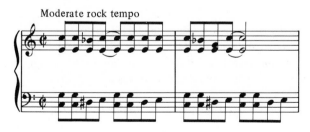

The percussion can be used to accompany almost any popular song. There is an undoubted gain in having a rhythm section performing and it is worth launching directly into a song that the class know and like, once they can play reliably.

It is not possible in a full classroom to teach everyone to play the drum kit, but everyone can be taken through a programme of games and exercises encouraging rhythmic independence of hands and feet and given some chance to try their skills out. Nobody has any difficulty in tapping left/right/left/right with their feet. How many pupils can perform the following pattern with ease?

Reverse the pattern, playing the four crotchets with the left foot. Play the pattern through four times (that is, four bars), reverse the pattern and play for another four bars. Pupils should constantly be required to perform these studies in the context of the bar and of particular numbers of bars; this develops more awareness of what is being done, and more thought has to go into time keeping. Applying this principle to the example above means that pupils should introduce a change in bar 4, the teacher counting out loud to prepare everyone for it.

Let the pupils introduce the left hand (slapping the table) in place of the left foot and, later, to coincide with the left foot. These should all be taken extremely slowly. Everyone should get them right however slow a pace they set themselves. They can increase their speed once they have a secure mental concept based on accurate performance.

Quaver patterns can be brought in with the hands in conjunction with crotchet movements with the feet:

Some of these patterns can be written on the board or directly into pupils' books. It is easy then, in subsequent lessons, to refer back to them and use them to reinforce basic knowledge. Example 2 gives some variations in common rock patterns which can be used in many combinations of hand and foot.

These are not all easy to perform and it is much better to use the most basic

Example 2

(notation)	RIGHT FOOT (BASS DRUM)
(notation)	RIGHT FOOT (BASS DRUM)
(notation)	RIGHT FOOT (BASS DRUM)
(notation)	LEFT HAND (SNARE DRUM)
(notation)	LEFT FOOT (HI-HAT CYMBAL)
(notation)	LEFT HAND (SNARE DRUM)
(notation)	RIGHT HAND (HI-HAT/RIDE CYMBAL)
(notation)	RIGHT HAND (HI-HAT/RIDE CYMBAL)

patterns when they are transferred to the drum kit. Some examples of paired rhythms for pupils to try are given in Example 3.

Example 3 (j) provides a good accompaniment to Fats Domino's 'Blueberry Hill'.

Example 3

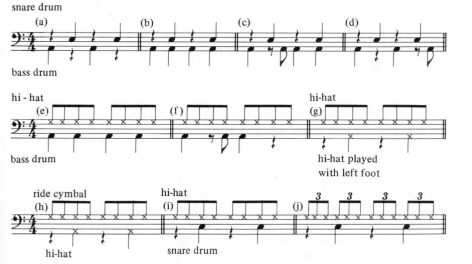

Pupils can hear the triplet figures on the record; the song has a conveniently slow tempo and can be used to explain what triplet figures are.

Pupils who have mastered some of these rhythms can be shown variations using the tom-tom. The tom-toms are usually reserved for 'fill-ins' – short breaks, of a bar or less, in semiquavers or semiquaver triplets, which are played in the last bar of a chord sequence, establishing a point of drama just before the sequence or a new section begins again. The break ends with a cymbal crash on the first beat of the following bar. A much simplified equivalent for pupils playing to a chord sequence or accompanying a song is to play a string of quavers, equivalent to the hi-hat rhythm, on the tom-tom (or split between the mounted tom-tom and the floor tom-tom) letting the previous rhythms drop for that bar. The point of greatest difficulty is resuming the old rhythm in strict time in the following bar. In notated form it would look like this:

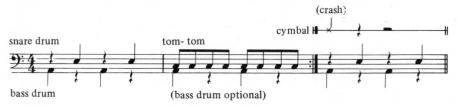

The bars can be practised separately until the difficulties of change-over have been overcome. The use of the tom-tom in this context is idiomatic and makes a welcome addition to the sonorities of the drum kit. Questions of sonorities are obviously difficult to bring up while pupils are learning to play basic rhythms. Nevertheless, different drummers will produce quite different sounds from the same kit, according to the volume at which they play, the distribution of accents throughout the kit, which instruments are used most and how the instruments are struck; this is a crucial element in the pop concept of music. Consequently, it is important to introduce pupils to the idea and effect of sonority at an early stage.

Balance of sound is something which can be brought out much more effectively in relation to a score: the scope of the rhythms is fixed by the score but the relative weight given to each instrument, the tempo and dynamics are all variables. Example 4 is a twelve-bar score for five players which gives scope for rehearsal and practice and can also be used as a percussion section with other instruments playing twelve-bar sequences.

One of the great delights for pupils in percussion work is to play along with a record. It is a good discipline in time keeping since pop and rock are played strictly in tempo. One LP I have used on many occasions is Fleetwood Mac's *Rumours*. It is not well known among pupils although four of the numbers on it reached low positions in the charts in 1977. It provides many examples of accessible rock percussion, clearly recorded. A piano reduction of the album is available for the teacher, who may want to have a copy of the words, the chord sequences and a quick source of

Example 4

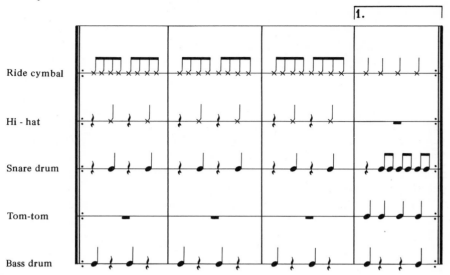

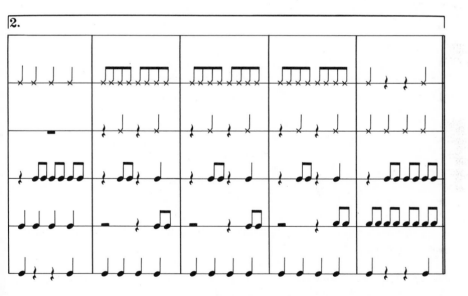

information about the organisation of each song. Pupils who have had enough practice in playing, listening and notating should be able to distinguish some of the differences in rhythm patterns between individual songs. 'Dreams' is a useful number
to start with: it is quietly sung, it has an uncluttered texture and a slow tempo. The
pattern is kept up consistently throughout:

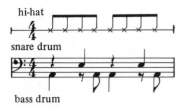

Pupils should come to know the song, with copies of the lyrics to help them see the division into verse, chorus, instrumental and coda. Two pupils can perform to the record in this way: one on bass drum and snare drum, the other on hi-hat cymbal and tom-tom. This second player will play the fill-ins and the cymbal crash (sometimes on the second, as well as the first and second, beat of the following bar, in imitation of the record).

'You Make Loving Fun' can be accompanied with the most basic pattern:

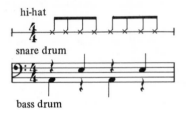

A variation here includes playing the hi-hat cymbal on beats 2 and 4 with the left foot, in addition to the normal quaver pattern with the drumstick. The bass-drum player can introduce either of the following patterns:

'Don't Stop' has more of a boogie-woogie character which is reflected in the hi-hat cymbal rhythm:

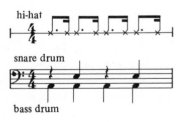

It is straightforwardly organised in four- and eight-bar units. The verse and chorus have an identical chord sequence concluding with two bars of the dominant seventh; it is easy for pupils to hear in sections which makes it a good song for practising fill-ins. The teacher can play through the sequence until the sound of it is aurally fixed:

I/♭VII	IV	I/♭VII	IV	I/♭VII	IV	V7	V7

There is much more subtlety to Mick Fleetwood's playing than these extracted chunks would suggest. Close listening to the record will generate practical ideas for variations and embellishments that can be used in the classroom, but there is obviously a point where, in classes of 25–30, keen pupils will have to look outside the formal timetable for their opportunities. Meanwhile there is enormous scope in the drum kit for activities which can start pupils on their way.

Latin American rhythms

Latin American and Caribbean rhythms are more complex than those of pop and rock and have to be considerably simplified for use in the classroom. They are more syncopated, consistently using off-beat accents. A greater variety of rhythms is used simultaneously and the variable sound qualities of each instrument are exploited more. There are more instruments, and many more types of instrument (struck, scraped, shaken, blown) than in the rock drum kit. Although earlier I suggested a minimal list of Latin instruments for the music department, there are several others, not too expensive, which widen the range of sound. I am thinking of the guiro, the agogo and the cowbell or, better still, a pair of cowbells. Though the expense is greater, it is preferable to buy a pair since, as with the agogo, very specific Latin effects can be brought out by splitting a rhythmic pattern between the high and low tones.

As in pop and rock styles, pupils should first become familiar with a number of basic rhythms. They should learn to read them as well as play them, transfer them to instruments and use them with musical accompaniment or in a percussion section in the performance of songs. Many Latin American rhythms are organised in two-bar units; these should be introduced from the beginning. Example 5 provides some basic rhythms which can be used for rhythmic imitation.

A rhythm chart such as Example 5 can be issued on duplicated sheets and used as a 'score' for sight reading. Pupils can play just one rhythm, or two or more can be played at the same time. These rhythms are not easy to read; the pupils must therefore have plenty of opportunity to hear them played, so as to develop an aural model of the way they sound. A good way to test pupils' sight reading is to ask them to reverse a rhythm – that is, to play the second bar first. This is a common practice in Latin American music, which has the advantage of clearly demonstrating whether pupils are actually reading, or relying only upon their ear.

Example 5

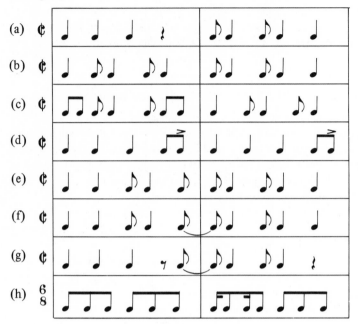

It is important to bring out the syncopation by strong accentuation:

Underlying the above accents is the first bar of the rhythm most typically associated with the claves:

Pupils can play this with proper preparation but I have not found pupils able to maintain it throughout the course of a full accompaniment. The following simplified version of the claves rhythm can often be used in its place:

As the notes and rests come in different places in adjacent bars, they still contain the surprise element. Other instruments can replace the off-beat accent omitted from the first bar.

Example 6 is a percussion arrangement for Harry Belafonte's 'Island in the Sun', showing some of these rhythms in use. It would do equally well for 'Jamaica Farewell', 'The Banana Boat Song' or 'By the Rivers of Babylon'.

Example 6

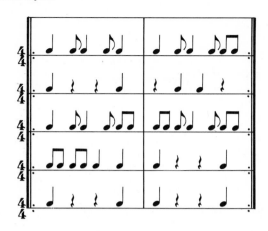

Maracas/hi - hat

Tambour

Two-tone wood block/agogo

Small tom-tom/bongos

Bass drum/large tom-tom.

Players on the two-tone wood block or agogo should change from the low tone to the high tone as the accompanying chords change. Since the verse and chorus both follow the same chord sequence, players will create a pattern such as the following:

Low	High	High	Low	Low	High	High	Low

Harry Belafonte's own version of 'The Banana Boat Song' uses a simpler accompaniment which can be performed in the classroom in the way shown below. The soft sound of brushes on the snare drum or hi-hat is much preferable to drum sticks in this style:

Snare drum/hi-hat/maracas

Bongos/tom-tom/tambour
Bass drum/large tom-tom

The studies in Example 7 are designed to prepare pupils for playing the bongos, tom-toms and conga drum so as to obtain a more authentic Latin American style. These instruments are struck with the hand, the fingers and the base of the thumb. The rhythms of the exercises are all typical of Latin American music, though they are simpler than the originals and more regular than the rhythms which drummers in the idiom actually play. It is worth mentioning that in a Latin American percussion ensemble the drums play a relatively free improvisation over set patterns laid down by the other instruments. Each type of dance has its characteristic unchanging basic pattern; this is always assigned to particular instruments, notably the claves and cowbells.

Example 7

(a) Instrumental rhythms

Bongos

R L R L R L R L

Conga

R L R L R R L

right hand

Conga

left hand

Cow bell

R R L R R R L L

right hand

Claves

left hand

(b) Dance rhythms

right hand

Baion

left hand

Afro 6/8

R L L R L L R L L L R

right hand

Afro 6/8

left hand

When practising these exercises, the class should be divided so that only a third of the pupils are playing them at any one time. At first, the desk top can be used as the 'instrument'; once pupils are familiar with a rhythm, they can try it out on the proper instrument.

These rhythms have to be practised slowly at first and, again, I think it is valuable to play each time to a regular number of bars with an accompanying melodic or harmonic instrument. As in Example 8, the rhythm of the baion (a Brazilian dance in a slowish two-beat time) could be played on the piano using a simple repetitive sequence to make up a sixteen-bar section. Pupils will quickly be able to pick it up aurally. A pupil on tom-tom or tambour can play an on-the-beat rhythm to keep the pulse steady.

Example 8

(IIm7+9)   (V7+9)   (I+6)   (I+6)

The Afro $\frac{6}{8}$ is a fine rhythm to use in class for improvisation because the basic beat is so definite. Humberto Morales (1954, p.87) gives twelve examples of variations that can be used for practising this rhythm alone. Siegfried Fink bases the whole of his percussion score *Caribbean Impressions* (1973) on it. Pupils find it easier to keep time, though not necessarily to play idiomatically, than with almost any other time signature. Two pupils should sit opposite each other and each play one bar in turn, one initially imitating the other's rhythm and then, later, each inventing rhythms in turn. The one-bar rest between each bout of improvisation is a useful device to provide thinking space. The teacher should initiate this exercise and there is no reason why eventually a number of pupils cannot join in, 'passing the rhythms round' in a small circle on a variety of instruments. Pupils very often get stuck with a tum-ti-tum-ti rhythm recalling 'Pop Goes the Weasel', 'The Miller of the Dee' and countless other songs of childhood and early school. Here are a few alternatives for use in $\frac{6}{8}$ time, which emphasise syncopation:

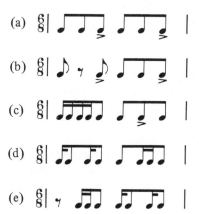

I have used the basic bongo rhythm, the claves and cowbell rhythms in a percussion accompaniment to Santana's 'Try a Little Harder Now' (Example 9).

Example 9

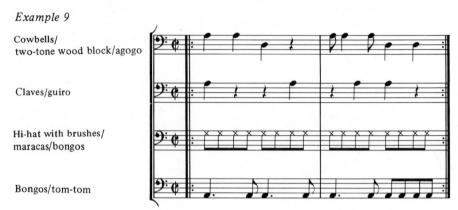

Cowbells/
two-tone wood block/agogo

Claves/guiro

Hi-hat with brushes/
maracas/bongos

Bongos/tom-tom

This song employs a battery of Latin American percussion generating tremendous drive and energy. It is organised in eight-bar sections, alternating a chorus, instrumental and verse. The chorus (Example 10) which is more of a chant, is simply a fourfold repetition of the phrase 'Try a little harder now'.

Example 10

Try a lit - tle har - der now

Am   D

The song uses only the two chords shown and it is not difficult for the teacher to improvise a piano or guitar part or for pupils to contribute with guitars (or an electric bass) to the harmonic side of the performance.

Rhythm and percussion work is sometimes thought to be an easier, musically inferior form of activity. In fact, I believe that it requires possibly the most rigorous concentration of any school subject. The appeal of it, though, is as much 'social' as 'musical'. Many groups of pupils I have taken have as much enjoyed playing the first 'Percussion Score' printed here (Example 1) as any of the others, although it is elementary to the point of not being a score at all. The satisfaction has been in the unity of the performance: the players starting and finishing together, playing in time and exploring the sounds of their different instruments. At whatever level of work these are surely the qualities to aim for.

References

Morales, Humberto, *Latin American Rhythm Instruments and How to Play Them* (Belwin Mills, 1954).
Fink, Siegfried, *Caribbean Impressions* (Simrock, 1973).
Fleetwood Mac, *Rumours*, Warner 3010(A).

Further resources

Adler, Henry, *45 Basic Bongo Beats* (Schirmer, 1957).
Brown, Ashley, *Play Drums Today* (Chappell, 1979). Basic introduction using original notation. Especially good in that each rhythm pattern is linked to actual songs, which could be used in class to demonstrate those patterns.
Evans, Bob, *Authentic Conga Rhythms* (Belwin Mills, 1960).
Fink, Siegfried, *Conga Brazil* (Simrock, 1974).
Fink, Siegfried, *Marcha del Tambor* (Simrock, 1973).
    The last two are actual percussion scores, eight- and six-part respectively, using LA/Caribbean rhythms. Useful for more advanced pupils, CSE, O or A level study groups. Knowledge of notation required.
Finkelstein, Mike, *Teach Yourself Rock Drums* (Amsco, 1979). Very thorough, more advanced study. Goes through the history of rock percussion styles from the 1950s onwards.
Leach, Joel, *Percussion Manual For Music Educators* (Belwin Mills, 1964). Nothing specifically on rock, though some material on Latin American instruments. Good on basic snare-drum/bass-drum work, gives simple exercises for these and for pitched percussion instruments. Good for general overview on percussion instruments, the names of parts, care of instruments, how to hold sticks etc.
Palmer and Hughes, *How To Play Rock 'n' Roll Drums*, (Alfred Music Co. Ltd, 1965). Basic introduction to rock styles. Most exercises and patterns linked to a twelve-bar format. Graded studies introducing bass drum, snare drum etc. in turn.

4   *Examining pop*

PAUL FARMER

Introduction

It is probably fair to say that, compared to other school subjects, music is generally
some years behind in its development of examination courses. In *Music in the Comprehensive School* (Farmer, 1979) I suggest that one reason for this was the tendency of public examination boards to assume that music will only be taken in the
later years of schooling by a minority of pupils with a specialist interest in the subject. The effect of this has been most extreme with O level exams, a form of assessment which even in popular subjects only affects approximately twenty per cent of
the school population. Where schools have confined their fourth- and fifth-year work
to GCE groups, their view of school music has as a consequence been considerably
restricted. This has tended to influence adversely the work done in the first three
years of secondary schools.

A major result of this concentration on GCE work has been the almost total
absence of pop music in fourth- and fifth-year school music courses, and often,
therefore, *throughout* the schools. In the Inner London Education Authority, for
example, there was only a token acknowledgement of pop in the Mode 1 CSE music
syllabus by the mid-1970s. During the same period the fact that very few Mode 3
music examinations were operating suggested that there was a reluctance on the part
of teachers to take the opportunity of changing this situation. Against this background it is easy to understand why the popular national press screamed such head-
lines as 'SCHOOL SWOTS GO POP!' when pupils from Holland Park school, London,
took the first CSE examination in pop music in 1976.

A CSE in pop

The fact that major changes in the examination system are currently proposed might
suggest that an account of work done for a CSE examination is now irrelevant. But
I believe that the project described is of value as an example of work successfully
undertaken and that in all essentials my findings apply to the implementation of any
examination in the field. When I was appointed head of music at Holland Park
school in 1974, the music department ran only the conventional O level and CSE
mode 1 music courses. Apart from a very small amount of group work with a syn-

thesiser, there was little 'serious' avant-garde music being performed, nor did there seem to be any pop or rock music which was officially backed by the department.

On arriving at the school I discovered that a large number of pupils had opted to take music during their third year, but that out of these only about a dozen wanted to take either of the existing conventional examination courses. This left a group of approximately thirty who had asked to take music (or who had somehow appeared in the music option, whether they liked it or not), but for whom there was no examination course. The only immediate solution to this problem seemed to be to arrange some kind of non-examination course which broke away from the traditional examination syllabus, especially with regard to musical literacy and 'classical' content. It therefore seemed obvious to base this course on pop. Almost all the pupils in the group were interested in some form of pop music (though their diverse interests *within* the pop spectrum later proved as difficult to manage as would those of a class of pupils liking both 'classical' and pop). A significant proportion already had instrumental ability and experience.

I should add that I had little knowledge of this field at that time, nor were there any materials then available specifically designed for school use.

THE EXAMINATION BOARD

It was at this comparatively early stage that I recognised the possibility of validating such a course through the local CSE Board (The Metropolitan Regional Examinations Board), and saw obvious advantages in doing so. It must be said that many of the pupils in this group were not highly motivated towards school work, and several were considered 'difficult' in other subjects; therefore the need for some kind of 'carrot' seemed important. A CSE course in this subject would, after all, provide an additional (or possibly only) examination certificate for the pupils concerned, and, though this was by no means the only reason for devising the course, its motivational value was not something I could ignore.

At this stage, however, the problems still appeared considerable. Not only had I to try to get a CSE course in pop accepted for the first time (as far as I am aware, no such course exclusively in pop had existed before then), but if it were to be within the reach of many of the pupils in this initial group it had to be practically based, or at least have a practical bias. For example, written work had to be kept to a minimum, so that those with literacy difficulties would not be penalised in the examination purely for that reason. At the very least there had to be a variety of ways of assessing work other than the conventional essay.

It was therefore with some trepidation that I approached the local CSE board with a draft syllabus (see below) and met with its subject committee in order to discuss this. I was very pleasantly surprised to find that there seemed to be no obvious prejudice towards the idea of a course and examination in pop, and indeed I found the Board, and in particular its examiner, helpful rather than discouraging. A principal concern, understandably, was the preservation of the standards of the CSE, and for this reason they were particularly concious of the relation of a Grade 1 pass to that of O level. Because of this they recommended that there should be a 'ceiling' of Grade 3 in the first year of the examination, for two reasons. First, familiarity with musical notation was not a compulsory part of the course, because this was a feature of the conventional Mode 1 syllabus which I had wanted to avoid. However, since the Board considered this an essential part of the Mode 1 syllabus, they felt that the two examinations could not be comparable in terms of these highest two grades. Secondly, they considered it safer anyway with a completely new examination to keep to the lower grades in the first set of results. I felt that the acceptance of the proposal was sufficient achievement for me to agree to this restriction, knowing that in the following year it could be amended in the light of experience (as indeed it was). In an article in *Music Teacher* (December, 1977) I set out guidelines for submitting Mode 3 proposals in music. In that article I pointed out that teachers interested in developing their own exams in pop should in the first instance contact their local examination board to find out details of the procedure for their own particular area. Typically, they will have to submit several copies of a syllabus similar in layout to the one given below, together with sample examination papers, up to three years before the first examination is due to take place. The proposal is then considered by a subject committee, who may possibly suggest alterations and improvements before accepting it. Further discussions with an examiner are then necessary in order to develop question papers and assessment schemes.

The following is an abbreviated version of the syllabus submitted to the Board. Reference may also be made to Farmer (1979) p. 65 where a comparison is made between this syllabus and others.

Holland Park School Mode 3 CSE Syllabus: 1977

1. PRACTICAL WORK

(a)   *Musical performance*
      Lessons are organised so that small groups of pupils can spend some teaching time playing instruments under the supervision of a visiting instructor. These groups leave the main class according to a rota. Those who have already learned instruments prior to the start of the course might play together as a duo or small group, while others are generally taught the guitar. All pupils are involved in some sort of music reading (see 2d).

(b)   *Recording/audio work*
      All pupils are taught the principles of recording, editing and producing a radio-type music programme, using a tape recorder, record deck and microphone. This activity takes place as part of the whole class lesson, during the time that those receiving instrumental tuition are absent.

(*NB: In the original 1976 syllabus, pupils had a choice of 1a or 1b.*)

2. NON-PRACTICAL WORK

(a) *History*
A broad outline of the development of popular music, from the beginning of this century to the present day.

(b) *Industry*
This covers the recording and manufacture of records, music broadcasting, pop journalism, the media and other related areas. Visits to radio stations and record company offices are organised, and visiting speakers from the industry are invited to talk to the pupils. Specific topics include: the development of recording equipment and techniques; the organisation and management of a performer; the marketing organisation of record companies; the disc jockey; 'bootlegging' and 'piracy'.

(c) *Listening*
Pupils are encouraged to familiarise themselves with the styles enjoyed by others in the group, and to listen critically. A note of opinions and observations can be taken where appropriate.

(d) *Reading music* (not included in the 1976 syllabus.)
Some time is spent teaching pupils to read music, or to increase their facility in doing so. This work is in addition to the experience gained in reading music when playing (see 1a).

3. THE EXAMINATION (in three parts)

(a) *Practical*
Two tape recordings lasting up to approximately 15 minutes each are submitted, having been prepared during the latter part of the spring term in the fifth year. The items can be recorded individually or by a group, providing the individual's contribution is easily identifiable. The tapes should illustrate:

   (i) performance on any instrument, individually or in a group; plus sight-reading exercises

   (ii) a short radio-type music programme, recorded, mixed and edited entirely by the pupils, who use their own choice of records.

(b) *Written*
In this 1½-hour paper, questions are set on the history of pop music and on the structure of the industry. These questions are drawn from the particular work covered during the preceding year (see 2a/2b), including areas dealt with only by visiting speakers. There are four sections to the paper, requiring, in this order, the following type and length of answer: multiple choice questions (ticking correct answer); one/two word answers; paragraph; short essay.

(c) *Aural*
Ten records or tracks are pre-recorded on to cassettes together with a short length of specially prepared music, played usually on the piano; this piece is

also printed on the pupils' question papers. Each pupil has the use of a cassette player with headphones during the examination which lasts for one hour. During this time the pupil's copy of the recording can be wound forward or back as necessary, and any part of it can be played without disturbing other pupils. The aural paper involves technical questions about the recordings on the tape.

ORGANISATION OF THE COURSE

At Holland Park we were lucky enough to have four good-sized practice rooms, in addition to the usual classrooms, and although the former were placed some distance from the centre of the department, they proved invaluable in housing small groups of pupils playing, where possible, under the supervision of an instrumental teacher. These groups were taken out in rotation from the main class, so that each had an equal amount of time receiving specialist tuition. The remaining pupils either worked with guitars, sometimes using the system devised for second-year pupils described below, or worked with recording equipment in preparation for their radio-type programmes. It would obviously have been useful to have also been able to put these groups in separate rooms, but this was not practicable. Nevertheless, although placing equipment in the corners of the room often proved hectic, this area of work was still possible.

In the 'history' and 'industry' parts of Section 2 of the syllabus, the main problem was lack of materials. In the mid-1970s there were no books on pop designed specifically for school pupils, and therefore it was necessary to start building up our own material from scratch. The school did however possess the EAV filmstrips on the history of pop, which provided a start, and though all these had previously been seen by the children more than once (as end-of-term 'treats', no doubt), it was possible to make use of them by designing supplementary material to go with them, mainly in the form of worksheets. *The Story of Pop* magazines were being re-sold at the time, and were also available in complete sets. These were an invaluable resource for the history section, particularly in the magazine form, since they could then be shared out among the class. They were supplemented with single copies of paperbacks, such as the *Rock File* books (Gillett and Frith, 1972–).

However useful *The Story of Pop* and other books were, there were two major drawbacks with this kind of material. First, the reading age for which they were designed was usually considerably higher than that of the class, and the style was rarely simple. Secondly, there were no activities, such as questions or exercises, which the pupils could be involved in. Therefore all the follow-up material had to be specially written.

Although to some extent the same approach to materials was possible for the industry section, the main resource here was visits and visitors. At that time record companies and radio stations had not been bombarded with requests for groups of pupils to visit them, and we were thus lucky enough to go on several visits. For a not only passed, but achieved Grades 1 and 2. I believe that they achieved a standard well beyond that which is normally expected of them, partly because they were assessed by a greater range of more appropriate methods than is usually applied in a more traditional syllabus, and partly because of a very high level of motivation, which the study of pop music is particularly suited to generate.

However, it would be wrong to suggest that there were no problems, either with this course or its examination. Some of these were teething troubles, and were able to be avoided in further years, but undoubtedly others were related to the nature of the course itself. For example, the assessment techniques could be improved and developed to a greater degree of sophistication and comprehensiveness; also still further opportunities should be presented for pupils at either end of the ability range to show their capabilities.

The above criticisms might well apply to an examination in any developing subject; but are there some which could be made of the very idea of a CSE course in pop? Firstly, there is a tendency for such a course to attract an unrepresentative mixture of pupils. What is required in any fourth- and fifth-year course is a mixture of abilities, where potential Grade 1 pupils are present as well as the least able; whether one then forms ability sets or not is another matter. But unfortunately, faced with a choice between a number of subjects, the able pupil (or his parents) may consider pop music too frivolous in comparison with, say, biology or German; yet other pupils may at the same time consider a pop course a 'soft option'. The result of each of these cases is a disproportionately high number of less able pupils, which *guarantees* one or more low ability classes.

A second criticism is that the pupil's view of music will be restricted by this course, and that what is required is a comprehensive course covering both pop and 'classical' music, together also with music from other cultures not yet incorporated into CSE Mode 1 exams. Such an argument certainly accords with my view of a balanced musical education, since I would not deny the need for pupils to encounter a range of musical forms. But such an aim is not met by most current CSE courses which deal almost exclusively with Western 'classical' music, and are therefore equally restricted. However imperfect a CSE in pop is as a separate 'subject', it seems to be the only way of ensuring that this area of music is included as a serious part of the secondary-school music curriculum. Finally, the course and examination described above can be justly criticised as being too narrowly conceived, even within the field of pop music. Many areas which could be incorporated into the course are neglected: there is no reference to electronic music, an area related to pop which is also rarely dealt with in Mode 1 CSE courses, nor is there any concern with the relation of pop to its historical and social context, of the type presented in *The Pop Business* or in the series of texts to be issued by Routledge (see Resources list below).

Pop in years one to three

THE THIRD YEAR

The success of Holland Park school's CSE in pop very soon influenced work in the school's earlier years. Before I was appointed, third-year music lessons had been discontinued, and so in planning a new course structure in order to re-introduce the third year to music, it was natural to consider how some of the CSE work might be adapted and included. Since the third year is the one in which option choices are made for the following year, this course was seen to be crucial in encouraging pupils to opt for the subject in the following year, when it was hoped that three courses could be run: O level, CSE Mode 1 and the CSE Mode 3 in pop.

Following the pupils' work in the first two years, which was uniform for all classes, pupils chose whether to take a pop or traditional course in the third year. Three classes were timetabled together and, from these, two pop classes and one conventional music group were arranged, the latter being rather smaller than an average class. In this group a certain amount of standard theory and aural work was done, partly in preparation for possible CSE or O level work in the following years, and there was also a good deal of practical activity, including avant-garde instrumental work.

The activities of the pop classes were similar to those of the CSE group with rather more written work than practical involvement, because of the larger number of pupils taking part. This meant that resources such as *The Story of Pop* were used extensively, with a set of specially prepared workcards, each of which covered a period or subject in pop, and which suggested particular issues of the magazine which could then be used.

The practical work was tackled by groups in rotation, with the assistance of the same instrumental teacher who had helped with the CSE groups. He was timetabled so that whenever the third-year music sets were being taken, he was able to take up to six pupils at a time to work with the electric guitars and a drum kit. His groups came according to a rota, thus giving everyone in these pop classes a chance to get down to some practical work for a limited period. Whilst there, these pupils would prepare a simple performance, from scratch in many cases, perhaps using a twelve-bar blues as a basis for improvisation. This only required them to learn three guitar chords, but involved the teacher in 'boosting' the performance from the piano.

Where possible, guest speakers were invited to the school, as with the CSE group (sometimes it was possible for one speaker to see pupils from years three to five in one day), though with large numbers it was difficult to arrange any out of school visits. A number of cassette tapes were also prepared, together with worksheets which went with them. Each of the two pop classes would have up to four or five cassette players with headphones, and copies of the various cassettes, so that there would always be a few pupils listening to music individually and writing about what they heard. This activity developed from the method of aural assessment for the

3   The contributions of Bill Haley and Elvis Presley to the early development of Rock and Roll.
4   Big Bands and the swing era.
5   How a recording is made.

PAPER II

Listen to the six pieces of music recorded on your cassette, and answer the following questions. The number of the question relates to the number of the track (question 1 is all about track 1, etc). You may re-wind or wind the tape as you wish, to listen to any part of the tape again.

Answer **ALL** *the questions.*

1   (a)   How many sections are there where only instruments play?

 (b)   At the very end of the track, which instrument plays a very short soft solo just before the final drum roll?

2   (a)   At the beginning of this song, the music changed in: volume/speed/style. Write down which is correct.

 (b)   There are four steady beats per bar in the introduction to this song. On which beat does the cymbal play?

5   (a)   Is this music in $\frac{5}{4}$ $\frac{4}{4}$ or $\frac{3}{4}$ time?

 (b)   Name the style of this type of music.

6

 (a)   What is the common name given to the structure of this piece of music?

(b) Some of the melody notes are often called 'blue' notes. Put a ring round any 'blue' notes in the music which is printed above.

(c) The guitar chords for the first line of the piece of music are G. Fill in the chords for bars 5 and 6.

(d) In the version of this piece played on tape, there are some 'fill-ins' played which are not actually printed in the music above. In which bars are these played?

(e) Fill in the missing final note of the melody.

APPENDIX 2: ANOTHER EXAMINATION SYLLABUS

John Comer planned a Mode 3 CSE course which was examined for the first time in 1980. His syllabus is defined in two dimensions.

In *content* he meets the requirements called for by Paul Farmer, since pupils are required to study the following set periods and topics:

Works for detailed study
1 Smetana: *Vlatava*
2 The Beatles: *Sergeant Pepper's Lonely Hearts Club Band*

Set periods and topics
1 The dilemma of modern music (Set work: Stravinsky, *The Soldier's Tale*)
2 English traditional folk song and the modern folk-song revival (Set work: *A collection of Ballads and Broadsides*)
3 From rock & roll to 'progressive rock' (Set work: Pink Floyd, *Dark Side of the Moon*).

As far as *skills and methods* are concerned, pupils are required to demonstrate various aural skills (e.g. recognise differences of pitch and rhythm) and to recognise excerpts of set works. Special attention is given to various types of compositional work (20 per cent of total marks) and to individual study (performance, or a written project, or making an instrument) (20 per cent). The certificate is awarded on the basis of both an examination and course work.

Musical theory and literacy are given relevance by being closely tied in with the study of the set scores. Typical questions might be (a) to give the meaning of the letters *ff* and (b) to give the chord symbol for a chord which is written out in staff notation.

John Comer's syllabus illustrates very clearly the truth of Paul Farmer's contention that popular music is suitable for presentation in an academic framework. His syllabus includes a statement of his intentions in terms of objectives (e.g. 'to recognise the sound of instruments and voices as defined in the syllabus'), and a weighted mark scheme, which is capable both of flexibility and of detailed specification (e.g. the answer to a question on 'the origins of progressive rock' must mention at least three of seven points given in the mark sheet used by examiners).

PART TWO
ASPECTS OF TECHNIQUE

Editors' preface

Though this section has a very important theoretical purpose, it should be stated at once that it is nevertheless highly practical. It is designed to help those teachers who are keen to use popular music in their teaching, but who feel they lack the competence to do so. It shows how classically trained teachers can, in the important areas of piano, guitar and vocal work, build upon their experience to acquire the essential concepts and techniques of Afro-American music – the principal musical impetus behind much contemporary pop and rock. Thus teachers who read John Comer's comments on the piano, for example, will not only find reflections on the nature of pop techniques, but also a large number of practical suggestions which they can both apply to their own playing and use as a basis for courses with pupils of all types.

One of the underlying purposes of this section is to raise questions of methodology. Naturally enough, we wish to promote our own philosophy, but we also want to take account of and reply to the very real anxieties teachers feel about the relation of work with pop music to the acquisition of a 'sound technique' or 'good habits'. Our view of 'alternative criteria' means just that – the acceptance of *different* standards of quality in *different* contexts, and not the acceptance of a policy of musical 'laissez-faire'. The standards for judging rock guitar or jazz bass are just as rigorous as those for judging a performance of a Mozart composition. Thus, where 'classical' norms are rejected, *alternative* norms must be specified to avoid music making which is not competent in any idiom.

In practice, as our contributors show, the differences are often more apparent than real. The classical pianist can acquire pop techniques as described by John Comer, and the rock guitarist can begin by following the methods of Elspeth Compton, without great loss or difficulty. What happens is the expansion of technical competence, and hence of aesthetic understanding and personal response. This is surely a goal to which we can all aspire.

However, such 'bridge-building' must not be allowed to obscure the essential differences which exist between any two traditions of music – this is as true of sixteenth-century polyphony and Romantic piano writing as it is of differences between 'classical', 'rock' and 'jazz' musics. We should not, therefore, automatically assume that the methods and techniques of one music are appropriate to another. And we make a plea that an investigation is needed both of the terminology we use (what is implied in a term such as 'good' technique?) and of the technical 'grammar' of Afro-American styles (what *are* the basic techniques of a rock guitarist?).

[71]

5 Rock and blues piano accompaniments

JOHN COMER

Rock and blues piano playing is quite distinct in style and approach from classical playing. I should say it took me two years to realise this fact, which now seems obvious, during which time I was perpetually on the hunt for *the* book which would explain the trick: how to use a classical training and the skills acquired over many years to play in popular styles. Book after book piled up but nothing much seemed to happen to my playing. Individual people would show me one or two things they knew on the piano, usually prefacing it with 'All you do is . . . ', confirming my belief that there was a trick to it, only I hadn't seen it yet.

A 14-year-old boy or girl learning a few chords from an older brother or sister, or trying to imitate a record that is in the charts, is, ironically, in a much better position than the trained musician, because there are fewer preconceptions and usually a much greater familiarity with the pop idiom, which has been acquired entirely by unguided listening. The young player's intention, initially, is therefore to reproduce the recorded sound as closely as possible and great pride is taken when this is done. Sheet music is often avoided since in many cases the person cannot read music. The keyboard is not conceived in terms of diatonic scales or even keys, but chords, chords which fit together by sound, according to the ear. Many of the chords used do not acknowledge the logic of tonic, dominant and supertonic relationships and the young person at the keyboard will effortlessly produce modal sounds – by using sequences of major chords moving in parallel, for example – and be unaware of the conventions of European harmony that are being disregarded.

In contrast, the classically trained pianist has special 'problems of transfer' in approaching popular styles which do not exist for the beginner. The following points seem to me to be the most important:

(1)   Problems of conception of the 'meaning' or purpose of popular styles, which are often mistakenly judged by classical criteria

(2)   Long-established habits of sight reading, and most notably, a concern for the 'exact reproduction' of musical scores. (The latter phrase obscures the fact that notation is generally used in conjunction with aural transmission, even in the classical field: much that is essential to the music is conveyed from teacher to pupil *by ear*. By this means vital conventions of music are also passed on, which consequently do not need to be made explicit in notation.) However, conventions of interpretation vary between idioms, and certainly between

[72]

classical and Afro-American music (see, for example, the note on p. 11). It is therefore possible to approach a piece of notation with a mistaken idea of the conventions which surround it, and hence with results fatal to the authenticity of the interpretation.

(3)   Unfamiliarity with the characteristic harmonic practices of blues and rock, and notably of harmonic parallelism, modality, the blues scale, crushed notes, and added fourths and sixths

(4)   Lack of experience in applying a different conception of the relative functions of the hands to that held by classical composers

(5)   Lack of experience of syncopation and cross-rhythm used as a basic structural element of the music

(6)   Lack of experience in implementing Afro-American criteria of rhythmic articulation, and notably its different patterns of accentuation, and its concern with effects such as swing, which are seen as crucial to the evaluation of the music

(7)   Lack of experience of improvisation as the dominant mode of music making, and of the criteria of Afro-American improvisation, which differ, say, from those used by a church organist

(8)   Difficulty in stepping out of the role of interpreter of notationally preconceived music into that of creator seeking to make a highly personal expression through music

(9)   A general tendency to conceive of the piano as a melodic and harmonic instrument (following the tradition of, say, Mozart) rather than as percussive, sonorous and colouristic. Alternatively, if familiar with the latter approach (for example, through the work of Bartók), a lack of awareness of the way in which, in different musical systems, the same mechanical activities are incorporated into different types of structure, for different aesthetic purposes.

If the above analysis is even partially correct, it is clear that Afro-American musical styles differ in a range of fundamental respects from those of the conservatory tradition. It is not therefore surprising that many pianists say they can't play in popular styles since they often haven't had either a formal or informal training for it.

Yet it is important for any teacher of class music to be able to accompany pupils on the piano, and if he or she intends to use popular music, it is both more convenient and more convincing if the teacher is free from total reliance on notation. Fortunately, the training of most music teachers includes some experience of memorisation, keyboard harmony, improvisation and related aspects of 'general musicianship'. In the following pages I hope to show that it is possible to build upon these experiences so as to obtain some competence in popular styles. In so doing I hope to provide a link between standard training and the more advanced 'introductions' to popular styles which are on the market (see list at the end of this article); I have found the latter to have limited value in the first instance, since they presuppose knowledge of the conventions outlined above.

The reader will find that, in traditional terms, popular styles do not require a high level of technique. But they do require a different approach, if they are to sound authentic. The teacher will find that the difficulty of acquiring this approach can possibly be ascribed to one factor, above all: *lack of familiarity with the idiom.* The one essential requirement for playing idiomatically in blues and rock (or indeed any other) idiom is an aural model of what the music is, and what makes it sound the way it does. This means serious listening and reflection upon and study of the style. But I am proposing that the teacher can begin by extending his or her existent knowledge along lines analogous to those hitherto used. (It is probably worth noting that the following materials can be used as a basis of a course for the pupils, too, though what needs to be emphasised may differ, because of their greater, though informal, knowledge of the music and its conventions.) I believe that the exercises will establish new physical habits of performance, and will lay the basis for the development of a personal style.

Harmonic approach; block chords plus bass line

Rock and blues pieces are based around repeating chord sequences of a regular number of bars (8, 12 and 16 are the most common by far), the most famous and useful of which is the twelve-bar blues. Chords, as harmony, do not have the same function or value as in classical music since the continuous repetition of the same sequence precludes the longer term tonal organisation, drama and suspense which the classical harmonic system made possible. The practical consequences for the pianist are that the short sequences of chords are relatively easy to memorise and after a while recall becomes automatic. Many songs use only three or four different chords and change chords once every bar so it is quite possible, with growing familiarity, to anticipate the chords being used in a song even on a first hearing.

The twelve-bar blues sequence, represented in three four-bar sections, looks like this. Each square represents one bar of common time.

I	I	I	I
1	2	3	4

IV	IV	I	I
5	6	7	8

V	IV	I	I
9	10	11	12

This is the harmonic skeleton: what gives it life and expressiveness is the great variety of left-hand patterns (which provide a stable rhythmic basis) and the cross-rhythmic right-hand figurations which constitute the 'melody', the attack and colour of the piece. Take the typical 'boogie-woogie' style left-hand pattern given in Example 1, as it would be used in a twelve-bar sequence. Notice that the sequence of notes which makes up the chord in each bar (I, III, V, VI in bar 1) is repeated for each change of chord.

Example 1

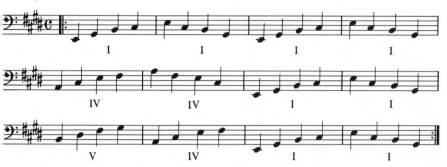

In a twelve-bar blues of six 'choruses' (a 'chorus' is the name given to the entire sequence played once through) this pattern would be repeated six times as written, though obviously individual players might introduce variations. The main variations in each chorus would come in the right hand and the variations there would be determined by whether the piano was taking a solo, the other instruments performing a subsidiary function, or whether it was playing the role of accompanist to a guitar or singer, adding splashes of colour here and there.

Initially it is a good idea simply to practise playing the appropriate chord in the right hand on the first beat of the bar so that both hands become completely secure in the knowledge of where the chord changes occur. It is common to have the tonic as the highest note and to play a three-note chord (Example 2).

Example 2

Having played Example 2 through it is very important to put the book down, if you have it in front of you, and play exactly the same thing in another key. It shouldn't be too difficult: the sequence of chords is known, the left-hand pattern using the triad plus the sixth note above the root is known, a suitable voicing for the right hand is known. Try another key. Try the right and left hand separately and then put them together. Aim for complete steadiness of tempo with no hesitation at the chord change in either hand. Try playing the right-hand chords on the second beat of the bar, accented and staccato. Try playing the right-hand chords on the second beat of the bar but split into pairs of quavers as in Example 3, using similar voicings for the subdominant and dominant chords. I think you will find that the basic format is beginning to take on some rudimentary life and character.

Example 3

Here is another 'walking bass' line to practise with (Example 4). I give the pattern for the first two bars only since the pattern for the other bars can easily be derived from them following the same principle.

Example 4

You will notice that the notes of the bass line in Example 4 make up the chord of the dominant seventh, just as the bass line in Example 1 made up the chord of the added sixth. Dominant sevenths and dominant ninths are an essential part of the idiom of rock and blues; they are used all the time to create a harmonic wash of sound but not with the expectation that they will resolve on to the tonic chord of a new key. A useful way of looking at this is to regard the chord sequence incorporating sevenths and ninths as a harmonic ostinato or riff: it is a colouristic background around which instruments weave a polyphony of motifs and melodies. Try using dominant sevenths on all three chords of the sequence. In Example 5 I add an extra chord on the fourth beat of each bar to give more substance to the right-hand

Try this pattern again, this time syncopating the bass line and playing even crotchets with the right hand:

When the syncopation falls in the same place in every bar the surprise value of it tends to disappear, and the pianist should always be looking for variations, found by experiment, which will become absorbed and used unconsciously. Example 9 gives two other patterns in which an anticipatory chord is played on the last quaver before the first beat of the bar. In both examples the two accented syncopated chords set up a cross-rhythm which should be strongly brought out. In Example 9(b) I drop the convention of tying quavers over within the bar and use crotchets instead since it should be clear what is involved in these displacements of accent. The use of the crotchet also implies that that note, being longer, should itself be accented, thus more accurately reflecting the rhythmic features which are characteristic of the style.

Example 9

(a)

(b)

With time and practice it becomes possible to vary these accents at will and achieve a proper fluency in their use. My experience is that, initially, it is difficult to change chord on the last quaver of the bar and to hold the chord there without playing it again on the first beat. These bars should be practised in different keys using the same voicings until the cross-rhythmic pattern starts to feel more regular and natural.

Improvisation

Learning to play in a popular cross-rhythmic style and learning to improvise are, to my mind, more or less the same thing for someone coming to the piano with already developed skills. They both require a different outlook on the instrument: the piano needs to be seen as a percussive, rhythmic source of sound and as the mechanism for releasing spontaneous and original inventions within the framework of a particular idiom. It should be clear that playing popular music involves from the very first the performer having to take decisions as to which bass notes or bass line to use, which chords and voicings to use and where and how often to displace the accents of the chords. Improvisation is not some special quality over and above this, although the word is frequently used in the sense of the improvisation of *melodies*. It is not a heaven-sent gift; it is a craft, an aspect of general musicianship which was taken for granted in the age of the thorough bass and which only became a specialism in the nineteenth century.

In all the examples I have given so far the voicings and the accompanying figures and motifs have remained approximately in the same register. One clear extension of the chord sequence is to vary the voicings and to do so in such a way that the top notes generate melodic interest and suspense. The first requirement is to become thoroughly familiar with the sequence, varying the voicings at will with no specific intention of producing a melody. Practise voicings with the root, third, fifth, sixth and flattened seventh notes at the top of the chord in purely impulsive fashion. It is not necessary to have every note constituting a chord to be present or present in every part of the bar. Notice from the start that it is impossible *not* to produce a melody or a decoration of sorts and that, because of the harmonic logic, such decoration may well sound quite pleasing. Be conscious of which notes of the scale you are using. Start each time with the root at the top, for example, and aim to finish on the fifth. If this doesn't sound final or satisfying start with the root at the top and finish the sequence an octave lower, taking care on the way to use again any particularly pleasing intervals or effects that come up. In a short time the random voicings will give way to a pattern that will be tune-like and, moreover, one that has been decided on by your ear and judgement. As soon as possible, you should try to have in your mind the sound of particular styles of piano playing, which you have heard on record and liked. Here are some examples of what I mean, with brief comments:

Plain chords with Caribbean-style flowing bass, suggesting $\frac{8}{8}$ time.

'Walking donkey' bass. Added-sixth chords implied by the bass and used in the right-hand melody. Light in texture.

Slower, ballad style. More cross-rhythmic, with chords tied over the bar. Fuller chords with basic rock bass.

Fast, blues/funk style. Dissonant major/minor thirds sounded together. Thin texture, repetition of notes.

These are just four permutations of one chord sequence; there are obviously many other chord sequences that can be used. Playing through these examples and playing similar types of pattern in different keys will fix them in your aural memory. However, such exercises should only be seen as a starting point; the details of what you play will and should depend on your judgement at the time of performance. In the first instance, though, the acquisition of such judgement can be usefully assisted by fostering appropriate (popular) muscular habits.

Interpreting sheet music

The interpretation of sheet music is a skill which it is important for both teachers and players to acquire. Sheet music arrangements do not accurately represent the music as it is played on record; but more than this, sheet music is actually misleading on occasion: the syncopated rhythms are often ironed out, producing simplifications which lack the true feel of the idiom. Compare the version in Example 10 of Lennon/McCartney's 'With a Little Help From My Friends' (*Beatles Complete* p. 202) with the song as it is performed on the album, *Sgt. Pepper's Lonely Hearts Club Band.*

Example 10

As you will hear from the record, the rhythm of these opening bars should be written as in Example 11. It is in fact represented in this way in other piano transcriptions and band parts.

Example 11

This is by way of illustration. The point I wish to make is that sheet music should be used largely as a framework, a means of finding out the words, the melody, the chord sequence in particular and any special harmonic features of the song and *not as a piece of music to be played as written.* Playing the song involves much more than interpretation in the classical sense; the piece needs to be re-created in whatever manner is suitable for the purpose at hand. What is important, if the song is being prepared for use in the classroom, is to know the original song before turning to the sheet music. Using the song album *The Beatles Complete* as a starting-point it should not be difficult to come up with a version such as the following:

Example 12

(variant for bar 4)

I have suggested a variant for bar 4, which leads into a repetition of the opening bars, to show another way in which the momentum can be maintained in the accompaniment while the melody has a semibreve. In bars 8 and 9 ('Oh I get by with a little help from my friends') the version in *The Beatles Complete* (p. 202) again gives a simplified melody with a plain statement of the chords (Example 13(a)) and I think it is quite justified here not to copy the melody line or rhythm exactly but simply to make use of those chords to capture the jaunty air of the song (Example 13(b)).

Example 13

key   Oh⌉
own?   No ⎬ I get   by with a lit - tle help from my   friends Mm, I get
nine   Oh⌋

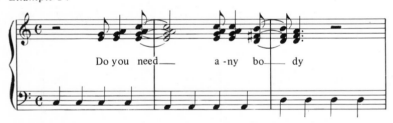

Similarly with the chorus: although the melody line is followed here it is the characteristic syncopation which makes for an idiomatic rendering:

Example 14

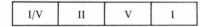

Do you need___   a -ny bo___ dy

The chord sequence for the opening four bars of this song is

I/V	II	V	I

which is easy enough to memorise. The melody line moves by step starting from the third degree of the scale. Knowing this there is no reason why you should not go to the piano and play these opening bars in a number of keys. Transposition becomes progressively easier as the harmonic relationships and their connection with the melody become internalised. The first new key is the most difficult; if you play it in all the major keys you will probably find that at the end you are virtually playing it without hesitation.

In bar 9 we come across the chord built on the flattened seventh degree of the scale (♭VII). This chord, sometimes followed by the chord on the flattened sixth degree (♭VI), occurs frequently in rock and pop and should be built into the harmonic vocabulary. For practice play 'What Shall We Do With a Drunken Sailor' armed with this information: there are only two chords – chord I and chord ♭VII; the verses and choruses are each four bars long using the sequence

I	♭VII	I	♭VII/I

the melody starts on the fifth degree of the scale and initially uses only the notes of the triad. Use any key, then try it in another. Play the chords alone at first and sing the melody. This will demonstrate that you can, indeed, play by ear – which involves a combination of knowing the song by heart and knowing technically how to produce the right sounds. It should also demonstrate that transposition, looked at from the point of view of sequential progressions of chords, is not quite the fearful activity that it is often regarded as.

'California Dreamin' by The Mamas & The Papas uses the progression

I	♭VII	♭VI

frequently throughout the song, as in the opening bar, for example:

Example 15.

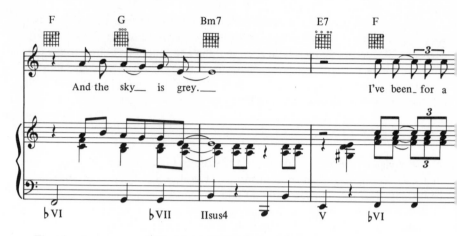

The chord sequence of the first sung section reads:

Im/♭VII	♭VI/♭VII	IIsus4	V7/♭VI

The flattened sixths and sevenths look more difficult notationally than they are in practice. They should be regarded as chords moving in parallel, using steps of a tone. This parallelism derives from the ease with which parallel harmonies can be produced using barré chords on the guitar. Practising a string of first inversion chords in the right hand on the two whole-tone scales makes these piano voicings much more familiar. The first two bars of the sequence printed above are hardly more difficult than 'What Shall We Do With a Drunken Sailor', consisting of the same effect but continued down one further tone. Overall, though, this is a more complex chord sequence than any we have looked at so far. The harmonic rhythm is quicker – two chords per bar generally and, to play it with style, more specific features such as the suspended fourth tied over the bar (bars 6–7) should be memorised. Here the suspension would lose much of its value if it became a middle note in a voicing. As with most sheet music, the piano line follows the vocal line; this is useful in teaching the song but it encourages a dependence upon always having the vocal line doubled on an instrument. In actual practice pop and rock musicians sing independent vocal lines over chord sequences. A possible voicing, playing this sequence simply as chords, would look something like this:

Example 16

so. The solution lies in appropriate pre-service or in-service training. Thus one purpose of this chapter is to act as a stopgap by indicating some of the main factors which need to be taken into account.

A further major problem for the amateur and the conservatory-trained teacher is lack of authoritative knowledge of popular forms and techniques. The ideal counter balance to this would be contributions from visiting professional performers.

EC: *The professional musician, who's making money by playing, and whose experience is in the real world, has a tremendous amount to offer the pupils.*

What sort of instrument should one buy?

First, a warning:

GA: *At some point the objects sold as 'guitars' in some of the big stores ought to be outside the Trade Descriptions Act – it's misleading to describe them as 'musical instruments'! . . . But in reality, especially in the less affluent areas, you often have to compromise. What else can you do if a child comes with a guitar which Uncle Joe bought her for Christmas, when the sort of instrument you'd recommend costs upwards of £50* [1981 prices] . . .

But if the teacher can choose?

FC: *The best you can afford.*

EC: *. . . a full-sized guitar. Small guitars are generally bad in quality and they won't stay on the knee . . . A full-sized guitar makes a much nicer sound. Children have got fresh ears. They haven't made the compromises that adults have about accepting poorer quality. Given a choice, children will choose the bigger guitar because the sound's better.*

And steel strings?

FC: *Not for beginners. The action is often far too high, and the strings bite into your fingers. Of course, after you've been through the basics you must have the right type of instrument, especially in the case of electric guitar. Otherwise the sound is not right, and there are things you just cannot do.*

EC: *If you're going to go for a steel-stringed guitar, you really must get a good one. With a cheap instrument, the sound is poor, and the action is too heavy.*

All the teachers were very aware of the physical problems which full-sized guitars present, especially to younger children. The main problems are the size of the body, the width of the neck, the height of the strings, and the distance between frets, especially up to the fourth position. No one was satisfied with the quality of small guitars, though Felix felt that manufacturers might try to remedy this situation if there was an obvious demand. With young children Elspeth uses a capo at the fifth fret. George was not happy with this and was concerned about possible confusion over pitch, note naming and reading. Elspeth recognised the importance of these comments, especially if you have a pupil with perfect pitch, but the risk was worth it she felt. She finds that there are few problems in practice. There are difficulties

EC: *. . . only if you give them those problems. As the children's fingers become*

able to cope, you move the capo back, fret by fret. The A follows the capo
back until you take it off for them. The problem is in your own mind.
Because it is not essential to have electric instruments in the first lessons, space dic-
tates that questions specifically about the various forms of electric guitar be left to
another occasion. However, three points ought to be made now:
(1)   At a certain point acoustic instruments will not do, because of crucial differences of construction, sound and technique.
(2)   The teachers were agreed that quality of instrument was again of central
importance.
(3)   Nowadays, amplification suitable for schools need not be a problem. Various
companies (notably Peavey) market amplifiers which produce a low volume,
but because of their design can nevertheless give the sustained sound favoured
by rock musicians. Such amplification is used by professionals for private
practice and for recording work.

Developing musicianship

All the teachers were very concerned that playing the guitar should not be a mechanical or isolated affair. They constantly stressed the need for the development of
theoretical understanding, the growth of aural skills, creative work and ensemble
playing.
FC: The one thing that has really encouraged them is getting involved in writing.
GA: If someone brings a song to you, however crude it is, you've got a starting
point. You've started by interesting them in music . . .

One of my primary interests at the age of eight or nine is not in turning them
into great guitarists but to get them musical through the guitar . . .

My task is not only to teach them guitar but to get them educated in the
language of music . . .
Elspeth is not quoted here, since the aim of fostering musicality so much shapes her
methods, which are described later in some detail.

Group work

All three teachers stressed the importance of group work. Not only does this reduce
the cost of tuition, but it inculcates musical habits of the most important kind.
(Individual lessons also have an important point part to play, of course.)
    Groups of four to eight pupils should meet in a room which is large enough to
permit the teacher to walk between them offering corrective advice. Elspeth prefers
pupils to sit in a semicircle:
EC: The sound is focussed in the middle – even with the open strings it can be very
exciting.
Felix has had to teach evening classes which can only run with a high enrolment of

fifteen or more students. He pairs them off after about six weeks to work on given tasks while he goes around the class. But despite the obvious limitations of the situation, many of the same advantages are obtained. Above all, one breaks down the potential isolation inherent in the instrument:

GA: *Get the guitarists out of their corners!*

An advantage of Felix' situation is that the pupils are often each other's best teachers:

FC: *There's a lot that I can remember that I learned just from talking to people of my own ability – just things that they picked up on and I didn't and vice versa.*

Elspeth had a great deal to say about the many advantages of group work:

EC: *They need the group experience . . . They get bored practising on their own . . . I think you produce better musicians this way . . . being aware of each other . . .*

You start right from the beginning insisting on correct ensemble playing – if they start raggedly, you stop, bring their attention to it . . . train them to count themselves in . . . 'subdivide the upbeat', as Gilbert Berberian would say . . . By such methods you develop their musical instincts – instantly it doesn't sound right they stop and say, 'Let's start again.'

They learn the discipline of working to a beat that is outside themselves rather than their own internal beat which is very flexible – they can slow down or speed up at difficult points. You want them to develop an internal metronome and an ability to count . . . Even after the first few lessons of group playing together, counting, getting that internal clock going, being aware of each other, being able to keep together, and if they break down or miss a note, not to start again but to pick it up with the others, to keep the flow of the music going.

The first lessons

Felix believes in teaching chords; this question is so fundamental that it is discussed separately.

George begins by asking questions such as 'What was the last record you heard?' He tries to find an existent interest in music on which he can build. He also tries to make every preliminary step an experience which leads to more general musical insights.

GA: *For the first few lessons, when they practise at home, they are so confused about what to do if the guitar goes out of tune. Especially as there are two notes called E. So you show them that the* thicker *the string, the* lower *the note, and the* shorter *the string, the* higher *the note. They really are fascinated by this. But if you get them to see how it works, you get at other principles too.*

As might perhaps be expected of a guitar organiser, Elspeth has worked out both her philosophy and her methodology in some detail. I felt it was important to give an account of her approach at greater length since, as she says:

EC: *These teaching principles are not limited to classical music, jazz or pop or whatever. They're concerned with what is essential to any music.*

Elspeth's methods

Elspeth's main technical objectives for the first few lessons are:

(1)   to ensure that the guitar is supported without any tension, and certainly not by the hands, which should be left free for playing

(2)   to bring about the acquisition of a firm *apoyando* sound (the finger pressing 'through' the string and coming to rest on the next string rather than plucking). This in turn depends on a relaxed right arm.

In brief, a *strong sound*, but a *relaxed arm*. The problem for the teacher is how to make this process both musical and interesting.

In Elspeth's view, one must seek from the very beginning to develop the young musician in four respects: performance, reading, aural training and inventiveness. But she feels that the *order* of acquisition is vital: first *doing*, then *reading*; first *imitation* by ear, then *invention*. In important respects this parallels work on language acquisition, which indicates that pupils should acquire some mastery in the oral use of language, before attempting to cope with writing.

Using the E (first) string only, the teacher plays a simple rhythm, for example a pattern consisting entirely of semibreves or minims, and shows how to count it out. The children have to listen, and then do it for themselves. The teacher corrects any right-hand faults. From the start the teacher can put an accompaniment behind the pupils' single notes, so that they can feel that they are playing a piece of music, no matter how simple it may be. As this accompaniment could be in any style, the method is applicable to the teaching of virtually any type of music.

As the pupils' confidence grows, the teacher increases the complexity of the rhythm to be imitated. Also the children are shown how the rhythm of what they know well is notated (pitch is not introduced in the earliest stages); exercises to reinforce this knowledge are introduced.

EC: *They can imitate quaver rhythms more easily than rhythms in minims. But slower rhythms are easier to read.*

These and any other processes need frequent repetition:

EC: *There is a difference between understanding intellectually and actually doing. In order to do something, you have to repeat it over and over and over until you've internalised it. The lessons are based on this kind of internalisation. You're doing the teaching; you're not showing them what to do and then expecting them to teach themselves at home.*

There is much to be learned even with these few musical materials. But when we add

the discipline itself? This question clearly relates directly to what we see the purposes of music education as being.

(4) *The teaching of notation.* The arguments for teaching notation are very strong, but are they to carry the day in all cases? The work of teachers such as Piers Spencer and Paul Farmer reported in this volume and in *Pop Music in School* suggests that premature or undue emphasis on notation may effectively shut out pupils with literacy difficulties whose musical talent is considerable and whose need for some form of school success is very great.

(5) *The 'chord or line' debate.* We would all agree with Felix, I believe:

FC: *It's so dangerous to misteach somebody something and to cripple them for life; it's a frightening prospect.*

Thus this topic is of central importance. My own belief is that underlying these questions is a more general one of what constitutes 'good technique'. This concept, and the actions we should take, can only be clarified by examining some of our underlying assumptions about what quality in music consists of, and by looking at the musical purpose of different teachers. This argument also applies to

(6) *The question of orthodox hand and finger position.*

(7) *The 'two instruments' thesis.* I believe that a resolution to the difficulties of points (5) and (6) is to be found by treating the term 'guitar' as though it were analogous to the term 'keyboard' rather than to the term 'piano'. Under the heading of 'keyboard instrument' we could list clavichord–harpsichord–piano–organ–electric organ–synthesiser. Clearly the techniques, possibilities, and characteristic usage of these instruments differ greatly, despite their basic similarity. A similar progression might thus be classical–flamenco–folk–blues–jazz guitar.

The above point leads me to my final remarks. First, the guitar needs to be properly researched so as to develop a methodology which conforms to the realities of what artists do, in no matter what idiom. Secondly, ignorance and prejudice need to be combatted and the willing helped by the inclusion of an appropriate course into teacher training. Thirdly, the account I have given suggests that, provided they are willing to look into the issues I have suggested, teachers can set about bringing the guitar into their schools with confidence. Not only can they do so, but they should be encouraged to do so, since it is an instrument for which there is a great demand, which is highly flexible, and of which the study can only advance the social, creative, and musical education of the pupils.

7 *The foremost medium – the voice*

ED LEE

> The important thing is to maintain the natural instinct to express one-
> self musically, and through the foremost medium – the voice
> (Neil Sorrell)

I have noted elsewhere (Vulliamy and Lee, 1981) that popular music can largely be
equated with popular *song*. Yet though a growing number of music teachers are
finding the value of introducing pop music into their curricula, and though there are
a growing number of books to service this need, no useful text as yet exists which
deals solely with the technicalities of popular singing. A first aim of this article is
thus to summarise some of the writing which does exist on this topic, and to add to
it two accounts of secondary school experience. One of these is by George Adie, a
teacher with substantial experience of working with professional popular singers;
his view of his task as a teacher is in important respects fairly traditional. The second
account, by Piers Spencer, describes work in vocal improvising with a range of pupils,
some of whom may find conventional forms of class singing uncongenial.

For some readers it may be a little surprising to link the word 'technicalities'
with pop singing. 'Surely', it is sometimes argued, 'pop singing is largely adolescent
drivel in a mid-Atlantic accent? Far from having technique, pop singers have little
but an affected manner and bad vocal habits.' The second aim of this article is to
combat this view, which is largely prejudice, is almost invariably based on little knowledge of or attentive listening to the field, and in which the concept of 'technique' is
based on a classical, instrumental model. This is not to condemn such a model, since
something like half of Piers Spencer's contribution to this article is concerned with
'scat singing', the process in jazz of improvising wordless lines, which are very
strongly influenced by instrumental practice. But it is here argued that though pop
singing (like all other singing) can be described technically and analysed, and that it
is legitimate to apply the term 'skill' in discussions of it, the criteria which need to
be used differ from those of singing as taught in the conservatory.

The structure of this chapter is therefore as follows:

The 'grammar' of popular singing. I suggest factors to take into account when analysing this music.

Ethnomusicology and vocal styles. Neil Sorrell gives useful insights into how to approach the music described in Part Three (Ethnic Music). But it is included here because of our conviction that the ethnomusicologist's approach can be extremely valuable to those who deal with popular music, and especially Afro-American music (i.e. the black New World tradition). In particular, the ethnomusicologist seeks to describe and explain rather than to evaluate, and so may help us to find the 'grammar' which it is argued below that teachers need.

Previous writing. I give a brief summary of some previous work on teaching pop singing, with especial reference to small-group work.

Thoughts on 'can belto'. George Adie talks about 'technique', small groups and especially songwriting.

Vocal improvisation. Piers Spencer gives an account of creative work with (jazz) 'scat singing', (rock) 'melismatic ornamentation', and (reggae) 'toasting'.

THE 'GRAMMAR' OF POPULAR SINGING   ED LEE

As I have already indicated, a comprehensive description of popular singing in technical terms has yet to be written. Thus the teacher is obliged to construct an analytical framework for himself. The following notes are suggestions as to what factors should be taken into account when analysing popular singing. It is assumed that the understanding such a process brings will be analogous to that which the music teacher has gained of 'classical' music during his training. It would seem likely that some such insight is necessary if the teacher is to be able to have any confidence in making comments designed to foster the pupil's own awareness of musical processes. The ideas outlined below owe a great deal to articles written for the *Teacher's Guide* (Vulliamy and Lee, 1982) to the RKP *History of Popular Music Series*, to which work the reader is referred for more detailed discussion.

There is ample documentary and recorded evidence that the best popular singing is a highly skilled activity. Singers such as Bing Crosby achieved and maintained their skill by persistent, conscious effort over a long period. In the case of any skilled activity it is possible to list a set of criteria which are being followed. Whether these are consciously understood or not is immaterial; it is possible (like the ethnomusicologist) to observe the evidence. In the case of a singer in a standard style we can thus compare the result to, and evaluate it by, the work of those performers who are generally agreed to be outstanding. In the case of a school pupil, who is unlikely to manifest high originality at so early an age, it is thus reasonable to insist that the child first name the artists whom he or she most admires, and then compare his or her work with theirs, according to the criteria which they adopt. The process of working out what these criteria might be will undoubtedly be inestimably musically beneficial.

In the case of very original artists, one needs to modify this process slightly, since in one sense there is no previous standard of excellence. One task must be to listen to a body of the artist's work, so as to discover what criteria the artist has set him- or herself. Secondly, cross-comparison can be highly useful. To give only two 'chains of influence', one could look at the works of Johnny Ray–Mick Jagger–Rod Stewart, and Ella Fitzgerald–Cleo Laine–Joni Mitchell.

Though the main concern of this note is not to stress such an approach, it is clearly possible and legitimate on some occasions to describe the work of popular singers in terms of traditional 'classical' analysis (i.e. melody–counterpoint–harmony–orchestration–form–arrangement/composition). George Adie does so, and clearly to great advantage.

However, the application of these criteria alone to all forms of popular music will not provide an adequate basis for evaluation, and indeed in some cases will be positively misleading. This is very true of music such as the 'early blues' of Little Walter, or the 'soul' of James Brown. The reason for such misreadings is that, though it is (like all Afro-American forms) a fusion, music of the type just mentioned retains a high proportion of 'African' elements. Composers in these idioms can be skilled or unskilled, imaginative or boring, as in any other field, but the criteria by which they may be judged to be so are substantially different from those applied to conventional music criticism. As George Adie puts it, 'The use of repetition has its own problems.'

When analysing popular music we should therefore first be on the lookout for the influence of the black Afro-American tradition, since the first influences of the black man's culture were being felt by about 1840, through the minstrel show. The weight which we have to give to 'European' and 'African' elements will vary greatly, sometimes within the work of one artist. Elvis Presley's 'Love Me Tender' has a strong 'European' element, whereas his 'Hound Dog' is perhaps best seen as a derivative of the (black) blues tradition.

The work of Afro-American musicians is concerned with the exploration of and aesthetic expression through nuances of rhythm and timbre. It is in the rhythmic 'argument' and in alterations of timbre that the essence of the music is to be found. Additionally, any artist seeks a distinctive and overall tone; the individuality of sound of Bing Crosby or Rod Stewart is an important factor in the high esteem they enjoy among the popular audience.

From the point of view of the music teacher, it would be useful to have a classification of popular singers according to these and similar criteria (such as mode of voice production). It is to be hoped that the work of Lomax, mentioned below by Neil Sorrell, has given a useful foundation for such a task.

Two other points remain to be made. The first is that pop song does not essentially consist of works of art in printed (sheet music) form: it is a 'live' activity, and as such can usefully be regarded as a species of drama in many respects. We thus

113-22) gives a sensitive account of the development of musical skill in a particular pupil. Not least important about this work was the fact that the pupil concerned was otherwise of poor academic record. His progress is further described by Malcolm Nicholls (pp. 126-9).

As we see it, a crucial problem in teaching the solo singer is that of knowing what criteria to apply. In part, this is a question of approaching the pupil in ways which lead and direct, but are both personally and aesthetically tactful. The nature of this approach emerges, we believe, from the various accounts which have been mentioned. But as was discussed above, it is also a matter of having some idea of which technical criteria to apply.

Songwriting is seen by all the authors as being both a feasible and a highly desirable approach to encouraging pop (and any other) singing. The account by Piers Spencer just mentioned is as much an account of a songwriting project as it is of technical development. Tony Robins' chapter (pp. 155-6) describes a slightly more spontaneous and unaided evolution of songwriting talent in one of his pupils. Work by both pupils can be heard on the cassette tape.

However, in view of the importance given to the subject, and its obvious creative value to the pupil, it seemed worthwhile to return to the topic in this volume. George Adie's account is thus of work which is equally creative, and which takes account of the 'alternative criteria' view of the music, but which tends to apply a form of analysis which is more 'traditional' both in content and in method of implementation. He also relates his work to wider issues of musicality and instrumental skill.

References

Frith, S., *Soul and Motown* (Routledge and Kegan Paul, 1982).
Heilbut, Tony, *The Gospel Sound* (Anchor, 1975).
Rogers, D., *Rock'n'Roll* (Routledge and Kegan Paul, 1982).
The texts by Frith and Rogers are part of the Routledge and Kegan Paul *History of Popular Music* series.
Vulliamy, G. and Lee, E., *Pop Music in School* (Cambridge University Press, 1976; 2nd edn 1980).
The accompanying cassette tape can be obtained separately from the book by ordering it through booksellers or from Cambridge University Press.

THOUGHTS ON 'CAN BELTO' – AN INTERVIEW WITH GEORGE ADIE   ED LEE

(Comments by George Adie are prefaced thus: *GA*:)

Underlying all George Adie's work, including that with singers, is a very definite philosophy. It is highly critical in some ways, and yet positive; traditional, and yet capable of relating to Buddy Holly and David Bowie. Because of his stress on 'discipline', it seemed to me that he held views with which many teachers would sympathise, and which contrasted in important respects with some of the other approaches described in this volume, including my own. At this stage in the development of work with pop music it seems to me to be undesirable to advocate too narrowly conceived a line. I have summarised his views, which were given in a relatively unstructured interview, under the following headings: philosophy, technique and discipline, musicianship, small groups, performance and songwriting. The quotations are accurate, but the interpretations are my own.

Philosophy

PREJUDICE

GA: It's very evident that some teachers have not listened to the music which they criticise. It is equally true that kids will say 'I don't like classical music' without being able to name a single piece which they don't like. It cuts both ways ...

But the attitudes of teachers and those who appoint them can be very worrying. I could name a 'Head of Drama and Creative Arts' who has gone on from strength to strength, whose only comment when asked what sort of thing he wanted for a musical drama was 'Well, just sing!

Again, I teach student teachers the folk guitar, and the conversation in the first lesson often goes like this: 'How many of you have ever sat down and listened to a folk record?' The majority never have, and will reply, 'Well, I'm not at all fond of that stuff.' 'What are you doing here then?' 'Oh well, we might need it in the classroom.' You cannot go into this sort of work with a patronising attitude, thinking you're doing second best. You've got to be aware that singing in the folk idiom is a pretty competent and well thought out thing – think of Joan Baez, Judy Collins, Ralph McTell, or Paul Simon.

George's experience of the discipline of the professional world manifests itself very clearly in the following comments:

GA: The teacher has got to learn that it's not a question of whether he likes the music or not – it's can he teach it and how can he set about it ... The main thing about a piece of music is not whether you like it or not, but whether you can learn from it.

PUPILS' CONCEPTS OF SINGING

GA: Some of them see it as a cult identification thing, some as speaking a poem in tune. And again, it is possible to see it as using an instrument.

A teacher I know put on a record of Kathleen Ferrier singing 'Blow the Wind Southerly', saying that the class was going to hear a folk record. The kids just giggled. They expected someone to come on with a guitar and an American accent, and they got a beautiful contralto singing a beautiful song . . . They both have their place, but one requires a different vocal technique and concept of what folk is to the other.

Technique and discipline

George came back constantly to the theme that singing is a technique and songwriting a craft and that there is thus a need for a disciplined approach.

GA: A former pupil of mine, a very educated, professional man in all other respects typifies a widespread attitude. We took his song to a professional singer I know. He found it absolutely extraordinary that this lady could just look at the song that I'd written out, which he'd sweated about three months to write, and that I'd helped him harmonise. She just took one look at it and sang it at sight while making coffee with the other hand. But that was just the standard of professionalism which people like her expect.

Whatever style you sing, singing is a technique.

To have a 'nice voice' can be very misleading. . . it means that most people do not regard singing as a technique to be studied . . . it's part of the cult of the gifted amateur or not-so-gifted amateur!

It's part of the misleading impression that has been given in the commercial music world in the past twenty five years or so. . . and by some movements in music education. . . Anybody in any branch of show business knows very well that 'spontaneity' and 'naturalness' take twice as long to achieve as contrivedness. . . Commercial pop singers of the pre-rock era were on the whole more trained. Most of them accepted that technique did need to be acquired very carefully. . . It would be unfair on the kids to let them think that it is easier than it is.

When asked what types of factor came under his definition of 'technique', George cited such things as posture, breath control, vibrato, diction and understanding of chest and head registers, topics which any classically trained singer would raise. But many teachers do not have such training, thus:

GA: To many teachers the actual chemistry of the voice may still be something of a mystery.

Failure to observe the principles of vocal technique could be very serious:

GA: Any experienced person in show business knows that if you don't know how to use your voice, you ruin it by mis-singing.

'Bel canto' is not a bad road to 'can belto', but 'can belto' will significantly ruin you for 'bel canto'.

This led me to put George to the various ideas on 'alternative criteria' stated elsewhere in this volume, and the necessary pressures of obtaining motivation, which we had discussed in connection with the guitar. He recognised the significance of the latter point, but continued:

GA:　Do we work from the particular to the general, hoping that, in learning one particular style, we don't mess up the capacity for being able, ten years on, when the person's interest may well have changed, to deal with a more generalised form of singing technique? Do we say, 'You want to sing like Elvis. Let's see what he does'? That requires a given person to know the sort of technique that Elvis uses, and to have a pretty extensive knowledge of the voice as an instrument.

This obviously returns us to a recurrent underlying methodological issue. But the need for effort on the part of the would-be singer still remains. A few years ago, George worked on a project for the BBC in which some typical schoolchildren set out to create and record a pop song.

GA:　When these kids, who were all dead keen at first, found out what hard work it was to get something worthwhile on to tape, they lost interest.

On this matter, I would however like to add an interpretation of my own. To quote ILEA Guitar Organiser Elspeth Compton, 'if things are difficult, you're trying to do too much at once'. To me this experience could therefore indicate, in addition to George's point, the fact that those who conceived the project which George had to put into action had underestimated in various ways. They had failed to recognise the amount of experience and skill needed in creation, performance and recording of any type, and of the complexity of pop music in particular.

Musicianship

GA:　Get rid of the dictum that there are musicians and there are singers!

Anyone who's going to be a singer ought to be able to knock out a tune on the piano or the guitar. If a singer doesn't play anything, he should certainly go in for a great deal of theoretical study.

The training of singers on these lines should in George's view, involve the usual elements of 'musicianship' courses including the use of notation. Especial attention must be paid to pitching independently of an instrument. Apart from being 'unprofessional', to give a starting chord does not necessarily help the untrained singer. For example, George frequently finds that amateurs start Bob Dylan's 'Mr Tambourine Man' on the note G, the root of the starting chord G major (chord IV of the key); this is particularly true if the guitarist plays that chord in root position, with the highest note being G on the top string. The correct note to start on is D (the fifth of the chord but the tonic of the key).

George does not entirely agree with the tendency to reject solfa:

GA:　I have been doing a bit of it with my pupils and found benefit in it.

It should perhaps be made explicit that George does not *insist* on theoretical knowledge, or instrumental capability, though he strongly urges pupils to acquire

'The Streets of London' they often haven't thought about it as meaning any-
thing until you put in the expression . . . for example in his eyes you'll see no
pride, so how can you tell me you're lonely' . . . at first they shuffle and look
embarassed – they're not used to such deeply felt emotions as Ralph McTell
obviously must have felt . . . but after a while they get the point and start to
think more about their own lyrics – what they really want to say.

[on the image as the major creative force in a lyric] *My job as a teacher is to*
look at a song they bring, and to recognise that it's largely unoriginal – putting
it tactfully of course – and to find the two or three lines that are good . . . and
to get them to see an image through instead of drifting into the 'Baby, I'm
sorry' idiom . . . [he quotes a specific example] *The song began: 'If you were*
a planet I would be your sun.' Very pleasant and effective. Then came the
second verse! 'So if you say you'll leave me I'll be oh so blue.' . . . but I urged
them to follow through the image, and they quickly came up with things like
'I'll be your Halley's comet . . . your satellite . . . you shook me like a meteor-
ite'. . . . they then felt that the old music wouldn't do . . . but they decided on the
relative minor after a bit of deduction . . . I said, 'How are you going to get
there – pause – 'Through the dominant' – 'Which is?' – 'C7' [note the completely natural interplay between 'theory' and 'creation'].
We completely brought the song out, and their faces all lit up, they went away
. . . and practised like maniacs, and came up with a song which I now consider
would hold its own in respectable company.
As praise from a professional musician for a set of 'average' children in a 'roughish'
comprehensive doing 'pop', that seems a suitable point to end without further
comment.

VOCAL IMPROVISATION   PIERS SPENCER

Listen to George Gershwin's 'Summertime' sung by an opera singer on a recording
of *Porgy and Bess*. Then hear the same song interpreted by Janis Joplin, with the
rock band Big Brother and the Holding Company. A comparison of the two versions is very helpful in getting us to understand the different attitudes to the voice
shown in the world of classical music on the one hand, and the world of jazz and
pop on the other.

In the operatic version, the notes are sung with exactly the pitches and rhythmic
values that Gershwin gave them in his score; this is equally true of the orchestration.
The singer's tone is trained in the *bel canto* tradition – a pure, clear sound, quite distinct from speech, and with a minimum of vibrato. The singer conceives her performance as subordinate to the overall musical and dramatic form of the opera. It is
vital that she does not alter the melodic line, as the 'Summertime' melody will
reappear throughout the work as a thematic motif, sometimes heard as a subsidiary
part in the orchestral accompaniment.

The Joplin version is intended to stand by itself, without reference to the operatic context. It is an intensely personal utterance, and, in many ways, is a complete
recomposition of the original song. Gershwin's metre and harmony are remoulded
by the accompanying rock band, and Janis Joplin's singing constantly deviates from
the rhythm, melody, and even the words of the original vocal line. Her vocal timbre
ranges from a pure sound to an intense, breathy growl, with a great deal of vibrato.
There is much improvisation: where Gershwin uses a single note to a vowel, the
Joplin line flowers into melismatic patterns; throughout there is a sense of excitement at observing a creative act taking place during a performance.

In this contribution I wish to show that though they may not reach the degree of
excellence exhibited by singers such as Janis Joplin, schoolchildren can successfully
attempt improvisatory vocal styles. Three vocal styles to be described here may be
of interest to teachers wishing to get pupils to explore the voice as a vehicle for creative experiment: scat singing, melismatic ornamentation, and reggae 'toasting'. Scat
singing, in particular, lends itself well to use in the classroom. The other two styles
are more dependent on the special talents of individuals, but we should be aware of
their potential, nevertheless.

Scat singing

Scat singing is the use of the voice as the equivalent of an improvising instrument.
The singing is wordless, and the singer vocalises on either pure vowels or nonsense
syllables. The range of musical styles which use scat singing is demonstrated by the
following three recorded examples of its use, taken from differing periods of musical history.

(1)   'Creole Love Call' (1927) by Duke Ellington (*At His Very Best*, side 2, track
       2). This is an example of the use of the voice in early jazz. It features the
       singer Adelaide Hall vocalising wordlessly over an orchestral backing. The
       number opens in a gentle, evocative mood, with the vocal phrases sung in a
       pure, 'disembodied', *bel canto* tone. Gradually, the singer introduces an ele-
       ment of growl, and the new timbre finally dominates the improvisation. The
       polarities of vocal style encompassed in this three-minute piece are remark-
       able, and the effect is moving. Post-war European composers such as Berio
       have explored the idea of linking familiar vocal sounds with unfamiliar ones,
       and 'Creole Love Call' in a way, anticipates some of their experiments.

       The harmonic basis of 'Creole Love Call' is the blues. Adelaide Hall sings
       antiphonally with the band at the beginning, filling in the ends of phrases
       begun by instruments. Later, she sings a complete twelve-bar blues 'chorus' as
       a solo.

(2)   'Oh Lady be Good' by Gershwin, in the version sung by Ella Fitzgerald (1944)
       (*The Best of Ella Fitzgerald*, side 1, track 7). An example of virtuoso scat sing-
       ing in the fast, chromatic, and rhythmically aggressive style of bebop. The
       Concise Oxford Dictionary of Music (Scholes, 1964, p. 511) quotes a definit-

ion of scat singing: 'an unhampered musical figuration just barely held to the melodic line – the atonal exuberance of a racial melancholy'. That a standard work of musical reference should accept such a definition shows that the author can never have properly listened to scat singing. Far from being 'atonal', Ella Fitzgerald's improvisation shows a consummate understanding of the harmony of Gershwin's song. The surface ebullience of her performance is deceptive, perhaps deliberately so. A close hearing will reveal a well-constructed piece of jazz, comparable to a great instrumental solo by Charlie Parker or Fats Navarro, in which not a note is out of tune, not a rhythm out of place and not a chord misconstrued.

(3)   'The Great Gig in the Sky' by the Pink Floyd (*Dark Side of the Moon*, 1973, side 1, track 5). This contrasts sharply with the last example, and shows how attitudes to harmony in Afro-American music have changed since the bebop era. Whereas Ella Fitzgerald negotiated a rapidly changing series of chords, here the female singer improvises with great passion and fervour on a static pattern, consisting only of the chord of Gm7 alternating with C9. In 'Oh Lady be Good', the harmony is functional, that is, one chord progresses to the next, imparting a sense of drive, enhanced by the rhythmic impetus of bass and drums. The static nature of the Pink Floyd's harmony carries an implication of the Dorian mode, and the singer's improvisation, apart from a few chromatic passing notes, takes place entirely within that mode. The emotional power of her performance, which encompasses both calm and frenzy, is enhanced by the singer's percussive articulation. A full transcription of this solo, and of the other numbers on the LP *Dark Side of the Moon*, is published by Pink Floyd Music (1973).

Other examples of scat may be found in almost every jazz or rock style. There are even examples in reggae: Bob Marley sings a short passage of scat improvisation in 'Crazy Baldhead', a song from the Wailers' *Rastaman Vibration* LP (side 2, track 1).

Scat singing is the easiest kind of vocal improvising to try with pupils in a class lesson. It serves as an introduction to jazz-related idioms without being hampered by the limitations of classroom instruments. Recorders, melodicas and xylophones cannot bend and colour notes as the voice can, and all aspects of musical sonority can be involved, even in a very simple scat solo.

First one could ask pupils to make up vocal riff-patterns using nonsense syllables. This can be done with a whole class. The teacher leads with a vocal riff, for example:

Example 1

and invites pupils to add riffs to go with it. Some will only sing the same riff along with the teacher, but others may show a flair for adding independent ideas of their own. Trevor Wishart (1974, p.24) describes a musical game called 'Riff-raff', which is worth trying with a class if you're getting this kind of work going.

The next stage might be to divide the class into small groups to make up short compositions consisting of vocal riffs set against each other. Example 2 shows the kind of texture which will emerge. It was made up by three 13-year-old girls. Pupil 1 made up her riff first, and pupils 2 and 3 added theirs as the work proceeded:

Example 2

If this exercise proves sucessful, pupils could try singing scat solos over familiar jazz chord-patterns such as the twelve-bar blues (proposed in Vulliamy and Lee, 1976, 1980, p. 89). Initially, soloists should try to 'plug' the gaps in the phrases of the blues 'theme', for example:

Example 3

Once confidence has been gained with short phrases, a full-length solo of twelve bars could be tried. Adelaide Hall's solo in 'Creole Love Call' would then be worth playing to a class, to demonstrate the range of colour possible in a scat blues. Another splendid example of twelve-bar blues scat improvisation can be heard again from Ella Fitzgerald in the number 'Smooth Sailing', from the *Best of Ella Fitzgerald* LP.

The blues is not the only familiar chord progression to encourage fluent improvisation. Some years ago, Glenn Miller's 'Tuxedo Junction' 'made the charts' in a vocal version by the Manhattan Transfer (*The Manhattan Transfer*, 1976, side 1, track 1). This had a fine scat solo, and inspired similar extended flights from some pupils. Example 4 is a transcription of one by a 13-year-old:

Example 4

This girl had a confident, rhythmically aggressive approach, and a sense of melodic shape. In performing this, she used dynamics, vocal colouring, 'bent' notes and vibrato with boldness and imagination.

Scat singing lends itself to a variety of styles, and it is possible for a class to experiment with a variety of musical settings. For instance, the static Gm7/C9 patterns of the Pink Floyd number described above could be used as a basis for modal improvisation.

Melismatic ornamentation

A melisma is a passage of song in which 'one syllable flowers out into a passage of several notes' (Scholes, 1964, p. 362). This florid technique is a common feature of some of the more lyrical styles of jazz and pop singing. For instance, at the beginning of the Beatles' 'Hey Jude', Paul McCartney sings a plain falling minor third:

Example 5

Hey   Jude____

By the third verse, this has become a spontaneously graceful and ornate phrase:

Example 6

Hey_   Jude_____

I have found many pupils with a flair for this kind of vocal elaboration, in particular adolescent boys with light flexible voices, and a good top range. In Vulliamy and Lee (1976; 1980, p. 113–121) there is an account of the work of a pupil fluent at melismatic singing who gradually developed into a very competent songwriter of some individuality. It is not really possible to get this kind of improvisation going with a whole class in one room, but if the situation permits a more individualised approach, with pupils working in small groups, there is certainly scope for developing this form of vocal expression. For example, a group of three pupils from a CSE music class, a singer, a drummer and a bass guitarist, got together to compose a song during a practical lesson. The bass guitarist came up with this bass riff, which has the familiar stepwise chordal movement found so often in reggae:

Example 7

M.M. ♩ = 69

against which his friend sang this bold and ornate phrase:

Example 8

which they later developed into a complete song. This style allows for the development of a singer's sense of harmony and speed of reaction to the implications of
chord changes. The teacher, with a greater knowledge of harmony, can be of real
help in suggesting progressions to pupils which will stretch the ear and improve
fluency. At first, it is best to use only the simplest chord progressions; more adventurous ones can gradually be introduced. I have met one or two pupils who showed
a quite amazing facility for melismatic singing. Example 9 shows for comparison,
two different melodic configurations improvised to the same words by a 13-year-old
boy who had been given the progression I–VI–II7–V7 to work on. The example is a
transcription of two 'takes' of a recording:

Example 9

Melodic and rhythmic invention seem to go hand in hand here. The phrases begin in different parts of the bar, being approached, as it were, from a different rhythmic angle. The melodic shapes which emerge are most attractive, and there is a considerable variety of intervals used, including the striking leap of a ninth which opens Example 9 (b).

'Toasting'

The distinction between speech and singing in Afro-American musical styles is often less clearcut than it is in classical music. A contemporary rock singer such as Joni Mitchell will move with ease from song to speech and back again, often within the same phrase. Her song 'Coyote' is a brilliant example of this flexibility. The sung rhythms of jazz and pop, too, tend to be closer to those of natural speech. This is not to say that classical composers did not have a profound understanding of speech rhythms, but rarely in classical music do we hear the flexible rhythms of colloquial speech counterpointing with complete ease against the strict pulse of the instrumental accompaniment, as in the Beatles' 'All You Need is Love':

> There's nothing you can do that can't be done.
> Nothing you can sing that can't be sung.
> Nothing you can say, but you can learn how to play the game,
> It's easy.

There is generally an even greater flexibility in the work of black musicians. This has been ascribed to the influence of religious practices (see Keil, 1966). There are recordings, for example, of sermons by black American Baptist preachers whose impassioned delivery often crosses the border between oratory and singing. (A further musical element of these sermons is the responsive 'amens' and 'hallelujahs' of the congregations.) Reggae disc jockeys, the 'sound systems men' (see p. 134), have become in many ways the secular equivalent of the preachers, and the declamatory 'talkover' of early reggae has now become 'toasting'. Perhaps because it relates closely to and exploits the rhythmic qualities of Jamaican speech, many West Indian pupils who reject other forms of singing have found toasting a satisfying form of vocal expression.

Toasting can be entirely spoken, can be intoned on just two or three pitches, or can use the entire pentatonic scale. It is always done either to a live rhythm-section accompaniment, or to the 'B' side of a reggae single, which has the vocal track faded out. Example 11 was sung during a lesson, to the backing of a 'B' side which repeated this bass riff throughout:

Example 10

Against this, the boy who had brought the record along as his contribution to the lesson, chanted:

Example 11

Despite the apparent monotony (which arises from the attempt to convey on paper the 'feel' of a style), the music has a definite rhythmic flexibility, being the marriage of the natural rhythms of spoken Creole with a reggae beat. The singer is also following the harmonies implied in the backing.

Although one cannot actually teach toasting, one can, even in the classroom, create a situation in which those fluent in the idiom can have a chance to show that they, too, have something musical to contribute. A lesson in which a teacher gets toasters to show their prowess could easily fit into a course exploring a whole range of vocal possibilities, from the traditional to the avant-garde. (For further ideas on these lines see, for instance, Schafer (1970).)

As a postscript, it is worth noting the potential of reggae for developing creative work in language. In Aston (1978), an anthology of poems composed by pupils in London schools, there is a poem, 'Dreads in the Alley' (p. 108), which uses the vocabulary and rhythms of toasting. One West Indian poet, Linton Kwesi Johnson, has made an LP, *Forces of Victory*, in which he recites his eloquent verse over a background of reggae instrumentals, in the manner of a sound systems man. Finally,

Edwards (1979) has further helpful suggestions for teachers to develop the language skills of West Indian children.

References

BOOKS

Aston, A., *Hey, Mister Butterfly* (ILEA, 1978).
Edwards, V. K., *The West Indian Language Issue in British Schools* (Routledge and Kegan Paul, 1979).
Keil, C., *Urban Blues* (University of Chicago Press, 1966).
Schafer, R. Murray, *When Words Sing* (Universal Edition, 1970).
Scholes, P. A., *Concise Oxford Dictionary of Music* (Oxford University Press, 1964).
Vulliamy, G. and Lee, E., *Pop Music in School* (Cambridge University Press, 1976; 2nd edn 1980).
Vulliamy, G. and Lee, E., *Popular Music: A Teacher's Guide* (Routledge and Kegan Paul, 1982).
Wishart, T., *Sounds Fun: A Book of Musical Games* (Schools Council Project, University of York, 1974).

RECORDS

Gershwin, *Porgy and Bess*, Decca SET 609–11.
Janis Joplin, *Janis Joplin's Greatest Hits*, CBS 65470.
Duke Ellington, *At His Very Best*, RCA Victor LSM 3071.
Ella Fitzgerald, *The Best of Ella Fitzgerald*, MCF 2569.
Pink Floyd, *Dark Side of the Moon*, EMI SHVL 804.
Bob Marley and the Wailers, *Rastaman Vibration*, Island ILPS 9383.
Manhattan Transfer, *The Manhattan Transfer*, Atlantic SD 18133.
Beatles, *The Beatles, 1976–70*, PCSP 718.
Joni Mitchell, 'Coyote' from *The Band : The Last Waltz*, Warner Brothers K66076.
Linton Kwesi Johnson, *Forces of Victory*, Island ILPS 9566.

PART THREE
ETHNIC MUSICAL STYLES

Editors' preface

The incorporation of a section on 'ethnic musical styles' into this book has several aims.

First, we wish to present further highly practical (and for the most part very cheap) projects for immediate use in the classroom. The question of relevance to British children need not be theoretically argued, since the projects have been tried with and well received by pupils, especially in the second and third years of secondary schools. This is true even of the suggestions which might at first seem fairly impractical: for example, Felix Cobbson's suggestion that we should try a project combining African music and dance has been shown to work with pupils in a very typical comprehensive school on a housing estate.

Secondly, experience shows that these projects have relevance for pupils interested in jazz, rock and pop, particularly in the development of rhythmic skill and improvisation. Perhaps this is not surprising since, as we stressed in the Introduction, popular music styles and non-Western musics share many common characteristics, and many musicians have explored links between jazz or rock and Indian music, and between reggae and pop.

A third purpose of these projects is to present material which will appeal to immigrant pupils. We should warn that these projects are not a panacea: the state of relations between different ethnic groups is such that the introduction of this type of work has to be made with considerable tact. It may thus often be best, as Neil Sorrell suggests in his chapter on Balinese music, to introduce ethnic music by means of a form which does not have strong personal associations to pupils. But Piers Spencer's chapter on reggae gives hope that the problems can be surmounted with great benefit to teacher and pupils alike. It may be worth mentioning here that teachers who seek further guidance concerning black studies music courses will find the chapter 'Black studies' (Vulliamy and Lee, 1982) and Hebdige (1982) useful in this connection, as they were designed for this purpose.

A final, but by no means least important, aim of this section is to attempt to make a case for a general philosophy of music, through practical classroom projects. The editors have on various occasions argued that pop music can only be truly understood by adopting 'alternative criteria'. But once the step of attempting to understand a music in its context and according to its own criteria has been taken, it becomes possible to approach and enjoy a whole range of other world musics.

Such a step is necessary because of the degree to which we in Europe have hitherto tended to approach other forms of culture with preconceptions so deeply based that we have been unaware of them. An example of this problem can be given by mentioning our own heart searchings over the term 'ethnic'. In fact, no term is as

[127]

yet available which satisfactorily links music as diverse as the ancient classical music of Northern India and the fifteen years or so of Jamaican reggae. All the music we describe is rhythmic (though rhythm is not strongly emphasised in all non-Western musics), yet the term 'rhythm music' suggests dance bands of the thirties. The musics have in common a tradition of oral-aural transmission, but, despite the inter-dependence of classical music and written notation, here too oral communication has a significant role to play. Again, 'non-classical music' suggests an undesirable and unjustifiable polarity. Thus, because of the use of terms such as 'ethnic minorities', we were pushed into 'ethnic', despite a possible overtone of anthropology and 'primitivism'. We have to hope that readers will be less affected by the label than by the fact that here is music which can be as pleasurable to listen to and as worthy of attention as that of the great European masters.

The projects

All the projects have been tested in the classroom and in many cases with full-sized classes of average ability. In each chapter a clear statement of the relevant back-ground is given, together with guidance on how to run the projects, and a list of further resources including how to obtain instruments. However, except in the cases of steel bands and African drums, the simplest resources (such as clapping) and regu-lar classroom equipment (such as the Orff xylophone) are all that is needed. The projects are not expensive minority activities, and they are capable of immediate implementation. But the great practicality of the projects should not lead to the belief that this work is some kind of inferior activity to be turned to as a last resort by the desperate teacher.

Though each contributor enthusiastically attempts to build bridges between his or her subjects and the realities of the British classroom, it is also very clear that the work is capable of extensions which will tax even the most gifted pupil's technical aural skill and creativity.

References

Hebdige, D., *Reggae and Caribbean Music* (Routledge and Kegan Paul, 1982).
Vulliamy, G. and Lee, E., *Popular Music: A Teacher's Guide* (Routledge and Kegan Paul, 1982).

8 Background to West Indian music

GEORGE FISHER and PIERS SPENCER

General background GEORGE FISHER

There are now over a million people living in Britain who were born in the West Indies, or whose parents came from those islands. Sixty per cent are of Jamaican connection and forty per cent are from Guyana, Trinidad and Tobago, Barbados, the Leeward and Windward Islands, the Virgin Islands and Belize. The map (Fig. 1) shows the arc of these islands across the Caribbean sea for over 1,500 miles from Venezuela to the Gulf of Mexico. Jamaica, in the Western Caribbean, is about half the size of Wales, is the third largest island in the Caribbean and is over 1,000 miles away from Trinidad and Tobago.

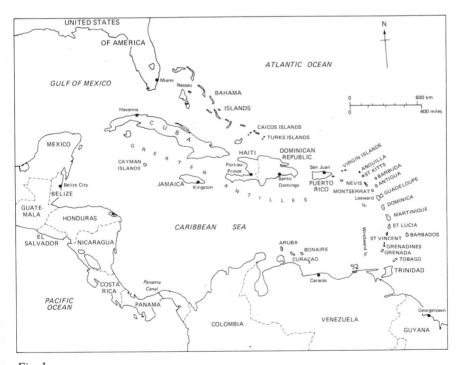

Fig. 1

The life styles and cultures of the people of Caribbean origin now living in Britain are linked by historical and social factors to those of the people of the West Indies, despite the distances involved and despite regional variations between islands. This is certainly true with regard to music. Moreover, in recent years the local 'pop' music of Jamaica has come to have an almost worldwide appeal, especially to the young, and notably in places where there are people linked by descent to Caribbean islanders.

Music is a cornerstone of life in many parts of the Caribbean; of especial importance are reggae and calypso. The roots of both forms of musical expression go back to Africa. Reggae has been influenced by Jamaican folk music and combines rhythms from this music and influences of popular styles of the USA with modern methods of reproducing sound. Calypso evolved from the West African folk tradition of making social comment through songs. The steel band developed similarly from African traditions of drumming, and grew in partnership with calypso. In both cases the annual Trinidadian Carnival was an important formative influence.

TRINIDAD

A brief description of the Trinidadian people and their origins will help to give a more detailed understanding of steel band music, the Caribbean and Caribbean music in general.

Trinidad and Tobago form one state with a population of over a million, largely of African and East Indian descent, and by religion predominantly Roman Catholic, Anglican and Hindu.

Though Trinidad has perhaps the most multi-racial population, the other islands are similarly of mixed race and reflect the same social structure. Divisions based on racial origin are accompanied by divisions into social classes based upon marked differences between rich and poor. All these divisions have developed from and are compounded by a history of colonialism and slavery.

The period of slavery began in Trinidad when the Roman Catholic Spanish were in control during the seventeenth century. The development of sugar plantations during this period necessitated a vast labour force which was obtained by enslaving and transporting large numbers of Africans to the island.

The emancipation of the slaves took place in 1834, and was followed by a period of limited freedom (the apprenticeship period) until 1838. After this many ex-slaves drifted into towns rather than work for former masters. As a consequence, Trinidad, along with Guyana, accepted a considerable number of indentured labourers from India during the second half of the nineteenth century. On Trinidad, between 1845 and 1912, 14,500 Indian labourers were recruited to save the sugar industry from collapse. Between 1853 and 1866 about 2,500 immigrants from China were also brought into the country.

The settlers brought with them their own customs and ways and the ethnic mix established by the migrations of people, in particular from West Africa and Asia, is still evident in the population today.

Despite the fact that in most of the islands mentioned so far the official language is English many stories and songs have been handed down from generation to generation in the Caribbean in *Creole*. Creole (also known as 'patois') is often referred to as a 'dialect', but is not defined as such by linguists. This is because creolisation is a process (found all over the world) in which two languages radically different in nature blend together into a third, distinctive form. Thus, Caribbean Creole is a unique form of English which was evolved by Africans when they were no longer able to use their native languages. Creole thus manifests many influences of African linguistic habits. In recent years, Creole has come to England with the people who migrated here from the Caribbean.

Creole has for centuries been the medium of an oral tradition. However, today, instead of passing on stories only by word of mouth children are writing and reading about Anansi the Spider Man and other folk heroes, and are listening to stories on records and cassettes. 'Anansi the Spider Man' is known not only to children in the Caribbean but also to those in West Africa, for he came from Africa to the Caribbean during the time of slavery. Recently, writers such as Louise Bennett, Linton Kwesi Johnson and young persons from the Black Ink Co-operative in Brixton, to name but a few, have been pioneers in using a written form of Creole. The recordings made by Paul Keens Douglas on his record *Tim Tim* are also becoming more and more well known. He uses Creole dramatically to describe larger than life but nevertheless relevant situations which are full of humour.

The lyrics of reggae and calypso music are often sung in a variety of Creole. Alternatively a Caribbean pronunciation is used, for example in the songs about 'Natty Dread' or in the calypso 'Little Drummer Boy' sung by Kitchener. Paul Keens Douglas' 'Sugar George' is a unique example of effective fusion of steel band music with an artistic use of Creole.

In nearly every area of Caribbean social life there are connections with life in Africa, apart from the linguistic. On Antigua for example, Warri boards are made. Warri is a game played in West Africa by moving small stones or large hard seeds between small hollows in the ground or scooped out from pieces of wood which have been fashioned.

Origins of the steel band   GEORGE FISHER

The history of the steel band has connections with Africa, with slavery and with reaction to colonial oppressors. On BBC Radio 3 recently, Alan Charles correctly described the steel band as 'part and parcel of Trinidad's invention and culture'.

Steel band is an invention of people of African descent. It was invented by people whose grandparents or great-grandparents were the sons and daughters of slaves brought to work on the sugar plantations in Trinidad by Spanish, French and British conquerors. At first, the African slaves were not allowed to participate in the

Carnival celebrations staged by the Roman Catholic planters in the days before Lent. When the abolition of slavery came in 1834, the former slaves began to participate enthusiastically, using African drums to make music. The Government of the time banned the use of the drums; in response, the ex-slaves adopted anything that would make a sound. Over the years a variety of instruments developed; one of these was the 'Tamboo Bamboo', made by cutting bamboo pieces into various sizes to obtain different sounds. During World War II the Tamboo Bamboos were stored away and began to rot, and when the Carnivals resumed people did not have time to make new ones. One of the objects that was taken up instead to make music was the oil drum, with the surface specially treated to obtain different pitches. Hence the modern steel 'pan' dates from the first post-war Carnival.

With immigration, the steel band grew popular in Britain; and by the mid-seventies, the Mighty Stalin had cause to sing in his calypso, 'Pan Man', to the people of Trinidad:

> Trinidadians are known as the creators of steelpan
> That is a world fact
> It established without a question
> But it is funny how they manufacture
> Steelpan in England and not from here
> Which is originally steelpan birthland.

Stalin was making an appeal through his song to 'pan men' and people of Trinidad. He wanted them to remember the importance of the Trinidad pan men and their contribution to the island's way of life.

Some of the pan men he had in mind, who were connected with the development of the instrument are:

Winston Spree, who died in 1976, often regarded as the founder of the movement;

Ellie Mannette, who divided the oil drum top into sections;

Tony Williams, who introduced the 'spider's web' arrangement of notes;

Bertie Marshall, who introduced such new ideas as canopies above the band stands and has contributed by developing the Bertfone pan, the quadrophonic pan and has been experimenting with the electronic pan.

More recently, we might include D. (Tweed) Joseph, a Grenadian now living in London, who has been experimenting with the electronic pan quite independently of his counterpart in Trinidad and has successfully developed the first and only electronic pan to be used in performances. The 'Pan Ogan' as he calls it is very versatile.

In Trinidad it has taken time for the pan men to be accepted, partly because many of them have not been employed in jobs except those relating to pan, and partly because it was in the poorer, crowded city areas where the music began. It has also taken time for steel band music to be accepted in England and there is still a long way to go yet. As long ago as 1951 the Trinidad 'All Stars' took part in the Festival of Britain, and enjoyed a success which helped the recognition of pans in Trinidad. By 1968 Trinidad had a special Adviser on Steel Band appointed to the

Prime Minister and in 1973 there was a National Consultation of Steel Band. By this time other steel band orchestras such as the Despers and the small family group known as the Samaroo Family Steel Orchestra were gaining an international reputation. Liberace for example, had employed a Trinidad and Tobago Steel Orchestra; the Trinidadian pianist Winifred Atwell had done so for many years. Winifred was one of the first professional musicians to combine steel band with the piano.

In Trinidad today there are about 200 registered bands and two kinds of pan men, the 'classic players' and the 'road players'. The classic players continue all the year round and the road players or part-time players come into action around Carnival time. Thus at Carnival time there are about 10,000 pan men in Trinidad and Tobago with an average of 65 members per band. For the rest of the year the 'stage side', or classic players, number some 4,000. There are more bands in the poor East Dry River area of Port of Spain, where the steel band started, than anywhere else in the country.

Most of the islands of the Caribbean have their own steel bands; this is true even of Jamaica which is the home of reggae. In Britain the steel band is now becoming part of the music scene. The followers and players of the steel band music in this country owe much to the dedication of the pan men in Trinidad. As Alan Charles says, 'Pan is the musical discovery of the century.' It was born in the slums in defiance of society and musical experts alike. It is a medium that can be used to produce a tremendous variety of music: folk, pop, or classical.

Reggae   PIERS SPENCER

Reggae is currently the best known musical product of Jamaica. It is an exciting new development in the Afro-American tradition, and has already had a great influence internationally on other popular music. However, unlike the bulk of popular music with which we in Britain are familiar, it is, at least in the form known as 'heavy' or 'roots' reggae, a music which is closely bound up with the political problems of Jamaica, the Rastafarian religion, and the problems of black identity and race relations both in Jamaica and Britain. These issues are too complex and sensitive to be given less than a proper coverage, which space does not permit. A few suggestions for initial reading on these topics are therefore given at the end of this section.

It is nevertheless worth allaying the fears of those readers who know of the Rastafarian movement, with its rejection of a white-dominated society and its institutions, including schools, and who may thus feel that its close associations with reggae militate against the use of the music by teachers. But it is important to realise that many children, both black and white, enjoy reggae as music for listening, for dancing, and for making themselves. The latter activity is a valid form of recreation which has enough musical content to make it educational as well, particularly when pupils of average ability are involved.

The origins of reggae can be traced back to the New Orleans rhythm'n'blues style of the 1950s, of which the singer and pianist Fats Domino was and still is a prime exponent. Music derived from this style, but with distinctly Caribbean features, started emerging in Jamaica in the early 1960s in the forms of ska, bluebeat, and later rocksteady. Reggae, which evolved around 1968, remains the most important style of Caribbean popular music.

Reggae tends to be disseminated by records rather than by live performances at dances or concerts. The records become known to the public through radio broadcasts, or through discos run by disc jockeys known as 'sound systems men'. Sound systems men have themselves made an important contribution to the development of reggae; they are often producers of the records themselves, and have developed vastly improved recording techniques since the music started. At discos, a sound systems man has a similar function to the 'caller' at a square dance, exhorting people to get up and move to the music. This calling is done through a microphone and mixed into the same public address system as the records. It was originally known as 'skank' or 'talkover'. The talkover had the quality of being half song, half speech, comparable to the talking blues of black American singers such as Leadbelly. It gradually developed into monologues chanted over the records themselves. This distinctive style of vocal improvisation is known as 'toasting'. It is the sound systems men, such as U Roy, Sir Coxsone and Tapper Zukie who are the big names in reggae, rather than the musicians who play in the bands. A band achieving fame purely as a band, such as the Wailers, remains the exception rather than the rule.

Despite the innovations made by sound systems men, the predominance of recorded music has had a rather unfortunate effect on the employment of musicians, and on performance opportunities for amateurs. There is simply less live reggae than there could be, and schools could play a part in changing the situation.

Further resources

BOOKS

Slavery
Craton, M., Walvin, J. and Wright, D., *Slavery, Abolition and Emancipation* (Longman, 1976).

Rastafarianism
Barrett, L., *The Rastafarians: Dreadlocks of Jamaica* (Heinemann, 1977).
Plummer, J., *Movement of Jah People* (Press Gang, 1978).

Jamaica
Kuper, A., *Changing Jamaica* (Routledge and Kegan Paul, 1976).

Black people in Britain
Pryce, K., *Endless Pressure* (Penguin, 1979).

Steel band
Elder, E. J. D., *From Congo Drum to Steel Band* (University of West Indies Press, 1969).

Reggae
Davis, S. and Simon, P., *Reggae Bloodlines* (Anchor, 1977).
Hebdige, D., *Reggae and Caribbean Music* (Routledge and Kegan Paul, 1982). (Part of the *History of Popular Music* series.)
Kallyndyr, R. and Henderson, D., *Reggae: A People's Music* (Carib-Arawak, 1976).

TAPES

The following tapes of radio programmes, produced by Vic Lockwood and presented by Dick Hebdige, are available on tape from the Open University:
Reggae: The Beginnings
Rastas and Rude Boys
The Sound System
They formed part of course DE 353 *Mass Communications and Society.*

9 Teaching steel band music

GEORGE FISHER

In the earlier 1970s there were probably not more than four or five primary schools which gave children the opportunity to play steel 'pan' instruments. Today, the number of primary and secondary schools with these instruments is in excess of fifty distributed over many Local Education Authority areas.

'Pan' was introduced initially by West Indian 'panists', enthusiasts, and a few Head Teachers with contacts in the Caribbean community. Underlying reasons were the belief that West Indian children needed cultural identity and the feeling that they had been presenting problems out of proportion to their numbers in certain schools. Although in a previous publication (Fisher, 1978) I have criticised the objectives of some Heads for introducing pan music, there can be no doubt that the music of the steel band can help to establish wider understanding about West Indian cultural development. The initial belief that the steel band music should be an activity exclusively for West Indians is now disappearing. There are a few all-white schools with good steel bands. This trend is encouraging as it is an indication that the cultures, arts and innovations of different ethnic groups are being shared.

It cannot be overemphasised that the presence of steel bands in schools has added a new dimension to the children's musical experience. Despite this, there are still many teachers and musicians who do not consider the steel band to be a serious form of music making. Pans are referred to as 'discarded old drums', as 'fun-Carnival music' or as 'bringing a ray of sunshine to the dull English weather'. Such stereotypes illustrate the difficulty pan music faces in becoming recognised in its own right.

Whereas the increase of pan instruments in schools is a hopeful sign, the growth of pan music in schools can present particular problems. This article offers some guidelines to those who intend to take up the challenge of establishing steel pan instruments in music education.

A role for the non-specialist

Firstly, the objectives should be considered. Is the aim to teach about Caribbean musical forms such as calypso or reggae, or is it to introduce steel pans as musical instruments? The relevance of this distinction is clearly connected with the competence of the teacher: in both cases expertise is necessary. In order to teach the musical forms, experience in Caribbean music and dance is a prerequisite. This would seem to rule out the possibility of most white English teachers making any significant contribution. On the other hand, such teachers can do a great deal to introduce pan to beginners. This only requires a willingness on the part of the teacher to learn something about the instruments. This is not an unreasonable expectation, since it is merely an extension of the principle that a music teacher is not expected to be able to play all the instruments of the orchestra or which are taught in the school, but rather to have an appreciation of their contribution to the total musical scene.

There is nothing to say that pan should not play English folk or pop tunes. In fact, such tunes as 'English Country Garden' and 'Grandfather's Clock' may be better to begin with. They are fairly slow and hence easy to manage, and do not require complicated 'sticking' techniques such as 'rolling' and 'dampening'. Also their rhythms are relatively simple. The enthusiastic teacher with some basic knowledge of music can cope with pan music at that level. In fact, by emphasising exploration, experimentation and creativity, the non-specialist can successfully teach the basic techniques of steel band music. All that is required is good organisation. Naturally, after the initial stages, as with any instrument other than the teacher's own specialism, an expert – the 'pan man' – is essential.

What are pan instruments?

The steel band consists of two sections: rhythm section and pans. The rhythm section comprises a range of percussion instruments – drum set, congas, bongos, selection of car hubs, scratchers etc. – and is similar in sound and purpose to the rhythm sections of Latin American music. The various pans, most of which are named after the voice or instrument to which their pitch ranges approximate (soprano, cello etc.), perform harmonic or melodic functions equivalent to those of conventional orchestral instruments. The basic kit recommended by many tuners includes:

2 soprano (also known as ping pongs)
1 double second (also known as tenor)
1 double guitar
1 triple cello
1 five-pan bass

The terms 'double', 'triple' etc. refer to the number of pans needed to cover the pitch range in question (the lower the range the more pans are required as fewer pitches can be obtained from a given surface area).

Though a few tuners suggest single seconds, these are not recommended as they are very limited in range. It is advisable not only to purchase the instruments from the same tuner but also to ensure that the tuner has a good reputation and a high standard of pan production. No two tuners produce identical instruments; the same tuner may produce soprano pans, for example, which vary in tone and sound because of differences of manufacturing process and 'styling pattern' (see below).

'D' SOPRANO/PING PONG (HIGH)

'C' SOPRANO/PING PONG (LOW)

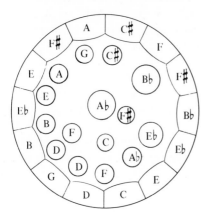

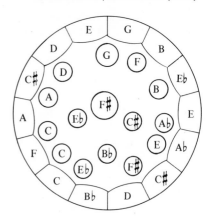

DOUBLE SECOND/TENOR

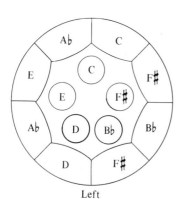

Left

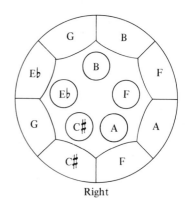

Right

GUITAR

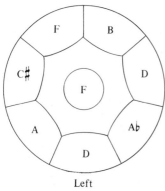

Left

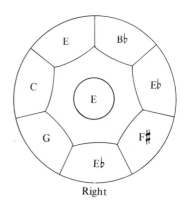

Right

Fig. 1

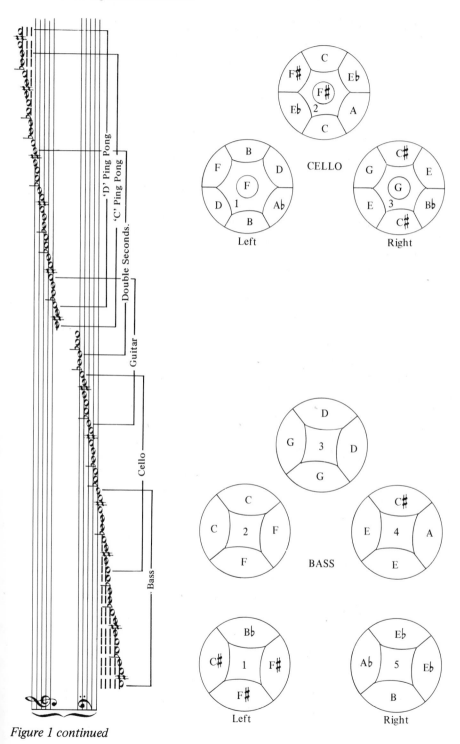

Figure 1 continued

In general, most tuners tune their ping pong, or soprano, in C. A 'C pan' means that the lowest note on the pan is C. Ping pongs may also be obtained in other keys such as C, D, E♭ , or E. A variety of tonal qualities will result in a richer band tone.

Styling patterns

The disposition of notes on pans (known as the 'styling pattern') does not follow a universally agreed system. However, a variety of styling patterns can have distinct disadvantages for the band sound, teaching and retuning. When the Inner London Education Authority (ILEA) took the step of becoming the first LEA in Britain to appoint someone with responsibility for steel band music, they though it necessary to adopt a standard styling pattern for all their pan instruments. Fig. 1 illustrates the patterns used in ILEA schools.

The patterns in Fig. 1 are not exclusive to the ILEA; they are patterns with which the majority of pan makers and tuners in Britain are familiar, and were in fact the patterns designed by the original Shell Invaders in the 1950s. It is worth noting, however, that in Trinidad other patterns are also used, which are claimed to be both more systematic and superior in sound quality.

The sticks

As the pan is a percussion instrument the 'pan sticks' are important. It is necessary that the right pair of sticks is used on the instrument. Pans must never be played with bongo sticks or xylophone sticks. The sticks should be approximately 1.2 cm in diameter, and should preferably be made of bamboo of the type gardeners use. Sticks come in three lengths (see Fig. 2).

The end of the stick which is to touch the pan should be wrapped in a rubber band of about 1 cm, or a little less, in width. For the ping pong stick (stick length 16-19 cm) the length of rubber band is about 10-12 cm, enough for three to four laps. For the double tenors and seconds (stick length 19-24 cm) a little more length of band is used to give a slightly fuller head. Though guitar sticks (stick length 19-24 cm) are the same length as tenor and second sticks, the rubber heads are made thicker. The bass sticks, which are 25-30 cm in length, differ in that they have a small sponge ball (or half a larger ball) at the head. It is a good idea to have a number of spare sticks ready as children have a tendency to fiddle about with the rubber on the sticks and therefore they undo them. In any case, at the outset, children should be shown how to wrap the rubber on to the sticks.

Another important stage in teaching pupils how to play is to show them how to hold the sticks properly. Teachers should impress upon children that the movement that is required comes from the wrists and not the elbows. In sticking the notes, the elbows should be kept fairly rigid and the wrists allowed to do the work (see Fig. 3). A useful exercise is to allow children to practise the sticking movements on the floor or on desks. Enthusiastic individuals may wish to carry their pan sticks with them so as to practise at will.

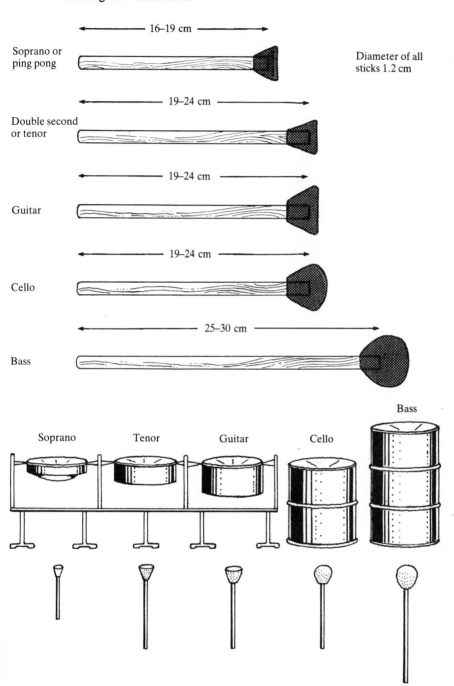

Fig. 2. Examples of sticks

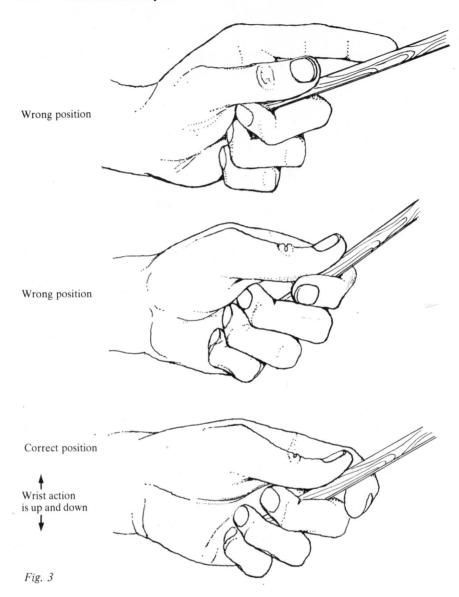

Wrong position

Wrong position

Correct position

↑
Wrist action
is up and down
↓

Fig. 3

Obtaining and maintaining pans

One question that is usually asked by those who wish to introduce pans into school
is: 'How do we obtain the instruments?' Another is: 'How much will they cost?'
Many LEAs are reluctant to finance steel band music in the normal way. Sometimes
they may feel that pans are not worth while, or that they are outside the main curriculum. But another reason for their reluctance is often that the instruments are

not yet obtainable through suppliers' catalogues. These tend to publicise instruments which, unlike those used in early music, or the steel band, are mass produced. Steel pans are not mass–produced because tuning is a highly skilled business. Thus pans have usually to be ordered directly from tuners and cannot be requisitioned through the normal procedures. The tuner will offer advice on the range that is required for particular needs. Delivery takes between four and eight weeks and sometimes longer, depending on the number of pieces ordered. Like most other instruments, the cost of pans varies according to who makes them and the quality of finish required. A soprano pan can cost anything between £60 and £200. As a guide, the cost of a basic set of fourteen pans is between £600 and £900. Added to this are the music cases and stands, though some schools can arrange to have these made privately. However, if cost or space make it difficult to obtain a full set of pans, a single soprano may be purchased and used in the same way as a xylophone in a tuned-percussion ensemble. Alternatively, schools may wish to co-operate and share a set of pans, as has been done in Leicester.

Clearly, steel band instruments need adequate storage space. A specialist music room is ideal. If space is limited the school may choose to purchase fewer pans; a four-piece bass can do the job almost as well as a five- or six-piece set. Alternatively special cupboards and racks can be built. Another possibility is to utilise the space under a stage. Whatever the storage method, the instruments must not be exposed to damp or to excess heat such as is found in boiler rooms.

As with any other musical instruments, pans must not be thrown about, sat on, or allowed to fall. When being transported, pans should preferably be cased up. They must always be played on recommended stands and not slung across chairs, nor placed on stools and benches. If they are stored and cared for properly, they will only need to be tuned once or twice a year. (My tenor has not been tuned for two years.) It is unwise for anyone except a professional tuner to interfere with the pans when they require tuning. This can result in damage to the instruments and a need for extensive repairs, as distinct from tuning, and can be very costly. If the playing surface of the pan is to be painted the tuner's advice must be sought. The underside of the pans must not be painted as this can impair the tonal quality. The rest of the pan may be painted or sanded to reveal a highly polished chrome-like finish. To avoid rust on the underside, a light rub with fine emery paper followed by the application of some motor grease, petroleum jelly or used motor oil is all that is necessary.

First approaches to the instruments

When the pupils come to use the instruments, they should ideally be standing above the pan in such a way that they have no difficulty in reaching all the notes. The playing position should not be erect and rigid, but slightly crouched. It is important that the notes are struck *gently*. The teacher should ensure that the left hand plays the notes on the left side and similarly that the right hand plays the notes on the right

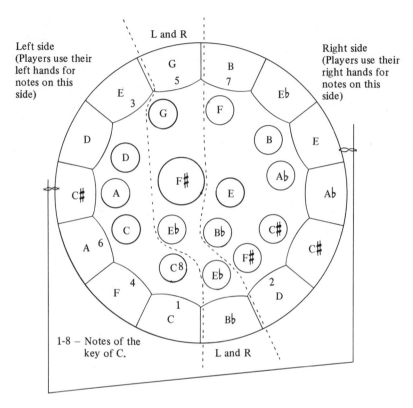

Fig. 4

side of the instrument. The children should not cross hands at the initial stages (see Fig. 4).

The construction of the pan requires the teacher to use a special approach when teaching the notes of the instrument, since the notes on the pan surface are arranged in a special pattern, and not from left to right as with the xylophone and piano. This pattern is more suited to the exploitation of the natural responses of a person using a pair of beaters, and ensures that both hands are used with equal dexterity and speed. At first glance, one may think that there is no system whatsoever in the placing of the notes, but in fact there is a distinctive arrangement for each instrument. It is important that children become aware of, and internalise, this arrangement. If it has been grasped properly, children should have no difficulty in playing with closed eyes. Certainly, partially sighted people who play steel pans seem to have no great problem in this respect.

In the first lesson some teachers get the children to play a scale – for example, that of C major. Others may allow them to explore the notes a little. There are a minority who would do what is *not* recommended, that is, get the children to play a tune first time around by marking the notes on the blackboard, and asking them to beat out the notes in order.

Pans with marked notes are common in schools. As a guide to the position of the notes this can be helpful, not least because the children tend to learn particular tunes more quickly. However, the marking of notes is not recommended, because it can have serious disadvantages. The danger of writing notes on the board and on the pan is that it emphasises the *visual element* in music to the pupil. Young learners can thus come to conceive of music purely as a set of automatic responses to visual cues, rather than as *sound*. They thus tend not to develop skill in listening, and become over-dependent on notation as a prop during performance. Moreover, experience has shown that children who 'stick out' the scale of C on a marked pan have difficulty in doing the same exercise on an identical pan which is unmarked. An experiment with a fairly competent 10-year-old soprano player, revealed that, whereas the child responded to the letters corresponding to the notes, very little attention was paid to the sound of the note. So while the child easily identified 'low C' marked on the soprano, she could not differentiate by ear the note of the same pitch on the second pan.

Another reason for not marking the notes is that such a practice tends to relieve the learner from making any real effort to form a mental map of the pan surface. Children should be able to form this mental picture, as it will enable them to play freely and quickly when necessary.

The 'sighted method', as I call it, can certainly make classroom control easier as far as the tutor is concerned. But it can also result in passivity on the part of the children, who become mere musical robots. It inevitably leads to an inability on the part of most children to play without the leadership of a teacher, or to try out ideas and to be creative.

A method which can go a long way to overcome some of the disadvantages of the 'sighted method' is what I call the 'discovery method', based on combining sight, listening and memory. Instead of using an instrument with 'marked off' notes, an unmarked instrument is used.

At first an unmarked pan face can make one feel at a loss. But this need not be so if the teacher takes a stick and leads pupils to find out by trial and error which note is where. After locating note C, for example, this can be written in chalk on the pan face. The children can be asked to find the note on their pans which sounds the same as the C played by the teacher; they are then asked to chalk it in. This process is repeated for the other notes. It may be argued that I have contradicted my previous warning since the class ends up with a marked pan face. The difference is that the children will have done the marking themselves, and have learned to distinguish different sounds in the process. Furthermore, the chalk marks can be removed to repeat the procedure whenever necessary, for instance when new groups are taken.

Other approaches to the writing down of the note names are possible. The lesson just described can be supplemented, in conjunction with the above, or at another time, by drawing diagrams of the pan(s) on paper. Alternatively, teachers may prefer to give out ready-made diagrams. Then, instead of writing in the notes on the pans, this is done on the diagrams, which the children can then use to find the notes on the pan.

Exercises

Having explored the pans and identified the notes, we may proceed to give the learners a few exercises to follow. Here are three simple exercises which can be fun and will enable learners to develop in music ability and in panmanship.

(a) *Chromatic scales*: In this exercise the learners work both individually and as a group, picking out the notes of the chromatic scale from the lowest to the highest and in reverse order. We can begin with the bass, followed by the cello, then the guitar through to the second and finally the soprano. In this way we can enable the children to follow the flow from bass to soprano so that they may appreciate where certain instruments feature within the range. Such exercises can improve dexterity, accuracy, speed and appreciation of pitch and range.

(b) *Diatonic scales*: The object is to get learners to become familiar with the scales and the keys. Sticking movements can be varied to include one, two, three and four beats to the bar. This can be done according to a rhythmic pattern if desired. Some teachers may prefer to get the children to follow all the notes of, say, C scale in order. However, a more exciting approach can be to make use of just five notes, the last of which becomes the first of the same pattern in the next key around the cycle of fifths, i.e.

This can be fun. There is an advantage in that children only have to remember at this initial stage five notes instead of eight. Also at an early stage they are learning to analyse the relation between the keys.

As in the previous exercise, all the instruments can be used consecutively thus:

Bass	C	D	E	F	G
Cello	G	A	B	C	D
Guitar	D	E	F♯	G	A
Second	A	B	C♯	D	E
Soprano	E	F♯	G♯	A	B

Obviously teachers should feel free to use any of the many variants of the above exercises which will spring to mind.

(c) *Chords*: The exercises given below are favoured by some of the best pan men. The idea is to get learners to take a creative approach to building chords. They should be encouraged to work as individuals, in small groups and to come together as a band.

The children are given a demonstration of the triads of the key of C, for example. They may be encouraged to note down the different chords, if desired.

C	D	E	F	G	A
E	F	G	A	B	C
G	A	B	C	D	E
				(F)	
I	II	III	IV	V(7)	VI
C	Dm	Em	F	G(7)	Am

These chords, and especially I, IV and V are the ones most used in the harmonisation of traditional pan music. The triad built on the seventh degree of the scale (B D F) is omitted here, since its use is virtually unknown, except as part of the dominant seventh chord. The latter may be taught at once, since its use is so widespread in popular music. Alternatively, the teacher may choose to add the seventh (F) as a separate phase in the course, so as to heighten the pupils' awareness of the effect of this discord.

As well as getting individuals to do these exercises, chords may be distributed across the different instruments from bass to soprano, for example:

bass	G
cello	B
guitar	D
second	G
soprano	Any two GB BD GD

Individual development and group work

A mixture of individual work and group exercises is necessary both to encourage a high standard of individual work and at the same time to relate that individual effort to the group exercises. In so doing, the children learn to co-ordinate their listening and sense of timing with that of others, a process which is clearly necessary for the smooth working of a group. This approach is important groundwork for the formation of a good steel band.

Exploring the pan surface in the way outlined will encourage some children to work out tunes that they know for themselves.

They will be able to differentiate between notes of the scale within the octaves, and between the sharps and flats. They will also come to develop sensitivity to tone on and between instruments. Inevitably such a method will mean a more lively and noisy atmosphere, but it will benefit the children. For a short time before the end of each session the pupils should all come together and even practise a tune.

Working in this way should enable the children to proceed with a minimum of supervision and leaders to emerge.

At the beginning, children should be encouraged to try all the instruments. After this exploratory phase, which lasts about three months, individuals usually emerge who show interest in and ability on particular pans. It is advisable that all children should be able to play the middle section, that is, the guitars, cellos and seconds.

There are nearly always more children than there are pans. In this situation it will serve no purpose to assign each child to a single pan. I observed a situation where a teacher allocated five children to each of the five bass pans. The five pieces which make up the bass must be played by one person only. This goes for the other sections of the orchestra as well. For example, one pupil should play all three cello pans. Where a teacher has a large group, pupils can take turns while others watch. Those not playing can draw and mark in pan surfaces, or practise sticking exercises.

Distinguishing instrumental timbres

Pupils should learn to play their particular pans, and learn to understand the part they play in the steel band orchestra as a whole. They should also learn to appreciate the function of all the different pieces in the band and be able to distinguish between them. It must be stressed that although the guitar pans and the cello pans are primarily used for chords and background purposes, they are different instruments, they sound different and will perform different functions. A common mistake many school steel bands make is to treat the middle section (seconds, guitars, cello) and even bass as though it consisted of one pan only. It may be satisfying to see the uniformity of hand movements of a row of children beating, say, the interval A–F of an F chord simultaneously – pa, pa, pa – on guitar, seconds and cello, but the result can be a most agonising noise. To bring out the real richness of these pans the chords have to be distributed appropriately across the pans and at the same time the striking movements have to be fitted into a suitable pattern which includes offbeats. As the children become familiar with the different instruments, they should be able to distinguish them by listening to good recordings. (A very good recording for this is 'Spanish Harlem' on *Chapter I* by Pan Am North Stars.)

Playing tunes

The tradition in pan music is to play by ear. In most cases panists play tunes which are familiar to them. Children too should be encouraged to play tunes that they know. Unfortunately, a few tutors introduce classical music (such as the 'Emperor Waltz') far too soon – within weeks of the children beginning to play. One school band produced an LP within a year of obtaining their instruments. Such achievements can serve to demotivate the children. The movements and techniques required to play classical tunes on pans are very advanced and it is inconceivable that in a short time young children could master them. Most important of all, some children give up playing simply because they are bored. They have not been allowed to experiment or to enjoy playing what they know. Instead, they have been coached and drilled into practising the same moves over and over again, especially if they have public engagements. Some Heads and tutors see nothing wrong with this and even some parents agree that it is a good thing. This is debatable. Certainly this orientation towards public performances should not be seen as the only purpose of learning to play the steel band.

It is not advisable that children should play together as a band before they have worked out their preferences for particular instruments and before they have acquired a functional knowledge of one or two of the middle-section instruments. The point varies at which an individual feels confident or is ready to play tunes together with others in a band. The formation of a permanent steel band within the first term of study can be premature. It can, as has often happened, give rise to tensions between children and sometimes between parents in the competition for places in the band. If the objective is to learn to play in the steel band and to make music, setting up a band too soon can be very counterproductive.

Preferably there should be a gradual move towards pupils working together in a band. One useful hint maybe to introduce the tune 'Doh re me' (from *The Sound of Music*) following on from the scale exercises. It is simple, easy to remember and, as there are no complicated sticking features (e.g. sustained notes), it is easy to play. It can be easily adopted to calypso, reggae or pop rhythms. It is an ideal first tune. If possible, suggestions for tunes should come from the children. They should be something simple and familiar to them, such as 'Brown Girl in the Ring' or 'Hallelujah'. Each player should be encouraged to hum or sing the tune first, and then to work out the tune on his or her own.

Rhythm

It is a myth that the black child has a natural talent for rhythm which others such as whites and Indians lack. A more acceptable theory is that the black child has been exposed to a particular form of rhythm, and that he or she has been socialised into it from the surrounding culture. So we find that most Trinidadians are able to dance the calypso beat. If other children besides those from the West Indian group wish to enjoy Caribbean rhythms and to learn how to make them, then they must be exposed to that kind of music. For example, very early on in their repertoire most school steel bands include a tune called the 'Peanut Vendor'; yet only a few of those bands maintain the consistent calypso rhythm which is required. Again, I know schools with steel bands but without a good selection of records. In the absence of recordings it cannot be expected that the rhythmic side of the children's steel band music will develop to any appreciable degree.

The first and most important step towards the development of rhythmic skill is to let the children listen to, dance to or tap to rhythmic music as often as possible.

In the case of the 'Peanut Vendor' they should at least be able to beat out the basic rhythmic pattern to the record before trying it on the pans.

It is essential to realise that the complicated rhythm of the calypso is a result of many individuals working together. Development comes by integrating rhythm and chording, and by getting the middle section to work out variations in sticking, as well as variations of the chord notes. A rhythm section with wooden blocks and chime bars, tambourines, bongos, old steel car hubs, graters and cabaça may be built up separately. Such work can be done effectively in the regular music lesson – for ideas see Chapter 3.

With younger children the jingle stick can be a useful addition. This is a stick (e.g. broom or mop stick) about 1½ metres long, on to which metal bottle tops are nailed at intervals (two or three tops to one nail). The bottle tops should freely move on the nails to make a jingling sound. A child then plays this by simply knocking one end of the stick on the ground or floor – a piece of rubber can be attached on to the end then floors do not get damaged and the thumping noise is absorbed. The jingle stick is preferable to tambourines at the initial stages, particularly for younger children whose wrists are too weak to handle the tambourine effectively. The jingle stick requires elbow and shoulder movements and so is much easier for the younger child to play. Also, the rubber attached to the end of the stick causes it to 'hop' slightly, which further reduces the amount of muscular effort which the child needs to make.

In all cases the principle is the same; as a rule, rhythm in Caribbean music is a result of the individuals beating their respective instruments at varied intervals and at varied speeds, for example:

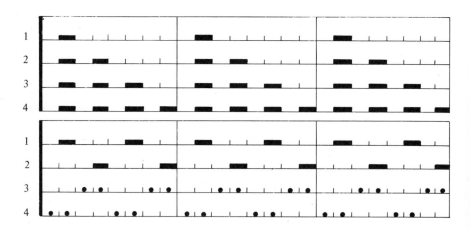

It is not necessary to have a tune to make rhythm. Anyone listening to West Indians knocking their beer cans at a Test match, will soon catch on to the idea of Caribbean rhythm making.

Conclusion

In a short article there must inevitably be areas left untouched and others touched upon only slightly. It is hoped though that those unfamiliar with the steel band will at least feel refreshed and stimulated by the above account. Certainly children will approach the instruments of the steel band with curiosity and excitement, though some children (especially juniors) will have difficulties, which they will overcome over a period of time.

For instance, as in other types of school activity, young children's concentration wanders; in the exercises for example, they are likely to need to change between instruments and exercises rapidly. One must also bear in mind that playing in the steel band can be very tiring, especially for young children who are not yet sufficiently physically developed. One must be careful not to drive them too hard, as some can develop muscle fatigue. The teacher should get them to take the work slowly and gradually to build up stamina as their muscles develop through practice.

Especially with younger children, teachers are likely to find that pupils will wish to play other instruments which they are studying, such as the recorder, along with the steel band. This is to be encouraged. The steel band was itself a creative innovation in making music in hitherto unknown ways. This process continues, as we can see from such inventions as the electronic pan. Thus pan music is not purist or exclusive; it is very much a social activity.

This leads me to my final point, which is that I have laid particular emphasis on individual development and group co-operation as two aspects of music making which should be seen as closely related. Music is a social activity. This sociality should be made explicit, but at the same time the individuals who make up the social group must possess certain skills. The balance between these two is crucial; too much emphasis on the group can be at the expense of individual competence. Similarly if particular players become too individualistic we can expect disunity among the group. As ever, the task of the teacher is to foster both individual growth and the ability to work with others.

Reference

Fisher, G. A., 'Beyond Yellow Bird', *Music in Education,* Vol. 42, July 1978.

Further resources

BOOKS

Elder, E. J. D., *From Congo Drum to Steel Band* (University of West Indies Press, 1969).
Hill, Errol, *The Trinidad Carnival* (University of Texas Press, 1972).
Prospect, G. A., *The Art of Making Steel Drums* (G. A. Prospect, Trinidad, 1970).

RECORDS

The following is just a selection of the large number of recordings available:

Big steel band sounds (Trinidad)
Barbados Steel Orchestra (1973), *Classics to Calypso*, WIRL W–042.
Casablanca (1973), *Steel Appeal*, Ashanti SHAN 101.
Despers (1974), Bach, Sibelius, Rossini (2 Vols.), Laventille Records CR 3180.
Despers (1977), *The Best of Despers*, Hildrina CO 3183.
Harmonites (1978), *Solo*, Romeys RSL 008.
Harmonites (1979), *Solo*, Harmony SH 667.
Hatters (1975), *Pan Champs*, LHS 222. Very good.
Hatters (1975), *Close up*, KDS 2007.
Pan Am North Stars (1972), *Chapter I* LRS 5007. An excellent record.
Starlift Carnival (1970), *Caribbean Sound Studios*. Very good.
Starlift (1978), *Panorama Champs (Live)*, ICE Records ICE 148

Sounds of the Caribbean
Steel Drum Jamboree, Request Records SLP 728. Features several big bands including
   bands from Antigua and Virgin Islands.
Tokyo, *The Caterpillar*, Compass CRS 0001.
Westland Steel Band, *The Sound of the Sun*, Explorer Series H 72016. Captures the
   sound of early forms of steel band music.

Big Bands in Britain
Ebony Steel Band (London), *Steel Away*, Line 2021.

School Bands in Britain on LP
BHSO (Broadheath School Steel Orchestra) (1978), *Harmony with Steel*, Peeping
   Tom Label HRSL 413. Obtainable from Broadheath School, Broad St, Coventry.
Ochorios (1979), Tank Label BSS 358. Obtainable from Tank Records, Welton Road,
   Warwick. Tel: 0926 45123.

Small Bands
Batti Mamizelle (1975), *I See the Light*, Essex Musical International.
Calimbo Steel Band, *The Heart of Trinidad*, GNPS 62.
Invaders (1977, LC 0366.
Magic Caribe, *Le Steel Band de la Trinidad*, Arion ARN 33167.
The Original Trinidad Steel Band (1969), Polydor 2489077. Excellent.
20th Century Steel Band, UAS 29878.

Poetry
Paul Keens Douglas, *Tim Tim*, PDK 001. Features poetry in dialect. An especially
   good track is about 'Sugar George', a pan man who practised constantly on his
   tenor to become a master at playing pan but, despite his talents, died a pauper.

SOURCES OF RECORDINGS

Our Price Records, 100 Kensington High Street, London, W8. Tel. 01 937 0257
Orbitone Records, 2 Station Offices, Station Road, Harlesden, London, NW10.
   Tel. 01 965 8292
Romeys Records (Distributors), Princes Street, Port of Spain, Trinidad
Woolworth Record Centre, Frederick Street, Port of Spain, Trinidad

guitar can be modified by use of a wah-wah pedal or echo-chamber. Other lead instruments in common use are saxophone, trombone and melodica, which is, of course, a standard classroom instrument. Instrumental virtuosity, however, is not valued for its own sake. The criterion of reggae musicianship is the togetherness of the *group* – each individual member has equal importance.

The vocal styles of reggae range from the aggressive, speech-like rhythms of 'toasting' to a gentle, floating melodic line favoured by girl singers such as Janet Kay or Louisa Mark. Backing groups of singers are often used and, as in rock and soul music, there are frequent antiphonal exchanges between lead singer and backing vocalists. (Some ideas for classroom work on 'toasting' can be found on pp. 124–6.)

Reggae material for the classroom

UNPITCHED PERCUSSION

First one can familiarise pupils with the percussion patterns found in reggae. A class can be divided into groups of three, and asked first of all to reproduce the pattern from Example 1, and then to make up a rhythmic ostinato of their own following the principles of contrast, clarity and economy. If a drum kit is available, it can be divided among three players, playing hi-hat, snare and bass drum respectively. The hi-hat cymbal should be kept closed with the left foot firmly on the pedal, and the edge of the top cymbal tapped with the tip of the stick to get a clean, clear sound. When proficient, the player can vary the sound by opening and closing the hi-hat between beats (Example 2). The bass drum should be padded with cushions or dusters to get the dry thud characteristic of rock music, and the snare drummer should experiment with the placing of the tip of the stick on the skin to produce the most ringing sound for his rimshots. Such a demonstration of the use of the kit could be given by three pupils, with the rest of the class watching, before starting the group work. It will not be possible for all to use the kit, and indeed a kit may not be available. However, the rhythms and contrasts of sonority may be obtained from hand percussion:

Triangle or sleigh bells	=	hi-hat
Claves or wood block	=	rimshots
Large tambour with soft beater	=	bass drum

by using home-made instruments:

Maracas (empty plastic bottle partly filled with rice)
Coconut shells
Upturned metal wastebasket hit with soft beater

or by using no instruments at all:

Hand claps
Finger snaps
Stamp right foot on floor

Pupils can be set to work on their two assignments for, say, 5-10 minutes, after which the teacher calls for silence in order to hear them. The second assignment, that of making up a rhythm using contrasted sonorities, often results in fresh and attractive patterns. Here is one made up by two pupils using objects found in their pockets as instruments:

Example 7

Player 1: Two coins tapped on desk

Player 2: Two pens tapped on desk

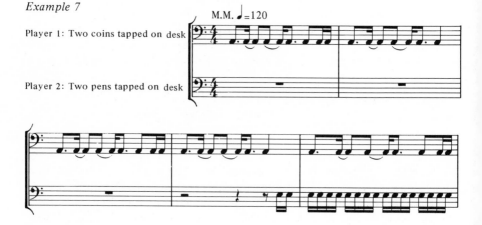

PITCHED INSTRUMENTS

A class with a good supply of pitched percussion can easily explore melodic and harmonic patterns typical of reggae. The use of xylophones is often something of a compromise, but in this case they can be used with total conviction, especially by pupils familiar with the idiom. This is because they are frequently used in West African traditional music, with which reggae has close connections. Here is a riff (ostinato) which could be played on a bass xylophone, or on the open strings of a cello:

Example 8

The chord of C is implied here, and the harmony is filled out by offbeat chords. Thus two pupils sharing a xylophone could play:

Example 9

Or two 'non-pianists' sitting at the music-room piano might try:

Example 10

First player

Second player
(one finger)

The offbeat feel of the rhythm may be beyond some pupils at this stage, and they
will need a little help in placing the chords accurately. On the other hand, abler pupils, who have grasped the offbeat quickly, may well be ready to elaborate on it.
Example 11 shows the offbeat chords on a xylophone broken up into a semiquaver
figure:

Example 11

A 'non-pianist' who can play a triad with one hand could be shown how to use both
hands to double the triad at the octave (see Example 5). Adventurous pupils have
gone on to try the full and satisfying sound of triads played with alternating hands
(Example 6). It is worth reminding ourselves that playing a triad, so commonplace
to us music teachers, can be a fresh experience even to a teenager.

A useful lesson would involve setting a class to work in pairs, learning to play a
pattern such as Example 9 on available instruments. The teacher should go round,
helping those with difficulties, and encouraging the quicker ones to elaborate.

It is now a straightforward step to start exploring the harmonic progressions common in reggae.

Example 12

This stepwise chordal movement is easy to learn on keyboard or pitched percussion, and is easier than the I–IV–V–I of the blues. Teachers need not be alarmed that the latter progression, fundamental though it is to so much music, is not learnt at this point: Carl Orff uses the stepwise movement of triads as the first stage of learning harmony in Vol. 2 of his *Music for Children* (1951, p. 74). Many modal folksongs can be found to imply stepwise chord progressions, and can be adapted to a reggae beat, for example, 'What Shall We Do With a Drunken Sailor?' Here is an arrangement for a whole class to perform together:

Example 13

reggae. Some of these are of great interest to pupils and can be reproduced in a modest way with school equipment. The information and suggestions given here may also be of interest to teachers who have smaller classes of older pupils doing music as an option either for CSE or as a non-examination subject. (The possibility of incorporating an imaginative approach to recorded music into assessed work submitted for CSE is illustrated by Malcolm Nichols in Vulliamy and Lee (1976; 1980), pp. 134–6, p. 178, and on the accompanying tape, Side 2.)

VERSION AND 'DUB' REGGAE

The 'B' side of almost every reggae single record is a fresh version of the 'A' side, known in the reggae world as the 'version side'. Frequently it is the same recording with modifications by the recording producer. For example, a sound systems man who is also a record's producer may decide to fade out the lead vocal track of the 'A' side, leaving only the backing vocal and instrumental tracks. The purpose of this is to enable him to replace the lead vocal with live 'toasting' at discos. The absence of a vocal track on a 'B' side appeals to many children, because it enables them to sing the vocal line themselves, or to improvise over the instrumental backing. The practice is similar to the 'Music Minus One' series of classical records, which enables the amateur musician at home to play a concerto accompanied by a record of the orchestral part only. The 'bare bones' sound of the 'version side' has encouraged some innovatory electronic experimentation, known as 'dub' reggae. Sometimes the musical material is subjected to a process of deliberate fragmentation. A few words or even syllables may be all that remains of the vocal part, and the individual instrumental tracks of the recording are faded in and out at will. The bass-guitar line, for instance, may vanish mysteriously for a few bars. Often echo is added, sometimes sparingly, sometimes lavishly, with the speed, delay and repetition of the echo subject to variation. Done artistically, these simple techniques can create a strange atmosphere with a kind of hallucinatory beauty unlike that of any other music.

An original 'A' side can yield two or three further versions. Here are two examples of recordings which exist in four different versions:

(1)   'Police and Thieves' by Junior Murvin (Island WIP 6316)
'A' side : original recording – vocal solo with a straightforward instrumental backing.
'B' side : the same recording with most of the vocal track removed, except for some cryptic fragments of words.
A small amount of echo added in places.

A few weeks later, another single was issued, 'Soldier and Police War' (Island WIP 6356), consisting of two further versions:
'A' side : a track of vocal 'toasting' by a disc jockey added to the original recording.
'B' side : the original recording with a saxophone solo added.

(2)   'I'm still in love with you, boy' by Marcia Aitken (LIGS 102)
       'A' side : original recording, a song with a sustained, chordal vocal track.
       'B' side : the original recording with some intriguing echo effects.

   A few months later, another single was issued, entitled 'Up Town Top Rank-
   ing' by Donna and Althea (LIGS 506), which incidentally, made the Top
   Twenty:
   'A' side : the sustained vocals of the original faded out and replaced by a more
   animated vocal track. ('No pop, no style, I'm strictly roots.')
   'B' side : vocal track replaced by an improvisation performed on a synthesiser.

Pupils involved with reggae are very knowledgeable of these practices, and show an
interest in trying them out themselves. The following could be tried:
(a)   Add a track of vocal improvisation to the 'B' side of a single. If the 'B' side is
       called 'Dub' or 'Version', this means that the vocal track is likely to have been
       faded out, and a pupil could mix in his or her own track of vocal improvising
       while the recording is being copied on to tape. Thus, using a stereo tape
       recorder, the recording could be copied on to the left-hand channel, with the
       new vocal track on the right-hand channel. The singer would need to monitor
       the single through headphones. A good example of this kind of improvisation
       is discussed in my contribution to Chapter 7, 'Vocal Improvisation' (Example
       11).
(b)   Add an instrumental improvisation in a similar way. A melodica, a saxophone,
       a brass instrument, or indeed any instrument could be used.
(c)   If the recorder has an echo facility, this could be used to add effects. Most
       recorders have rather limited echo facility, if at all, and the speed of the echo
       cannot be varied. For this a proper echo unit, such as a Wem 'Copicat' will be
       needed. One of the benefits of doing this work is that pupils learn recording
       techniques, and get a taste of the world of electronic music.

Reggae bands in school

Reggae is predominantly a recorded music. When teenagers go to a reggae dance, it
is more likely to feature a disco run by a sound systems man than a band performing live. This situation is not only bad for professional musicians, it also discourages
amateurs and children from making the music themselves. Over a period of five
years at my school, I encouraged bands to rehearse after school hours, and gradually built up a collection of equipment. Although the following observations are
written with reggae bands in mind, our equipment was used by rock, soul and jazz
groups too, and most of my remarks apply to any pop style.
   What is the teacher's role in fostering these activities? At first I felt that, as the
pupils knew the style better then I did, I had no other role than that of a store-

keeper, with a vaguely positive attitude to the music making! However, I have gradually learned ways in which a teacher can, and indeed must help:

(a) *Intonation*. The tuning of instruments should be checked at the beginning of a practice, and pupils should be encouraged to learn to tune the instruments themselves.

(b) *Balance and checking of sound levels*. A teacher can help groups find levels of amplification suitable to a really clear overall sound. He can give simple tips such as advising singers to stand holding their microphones *behind* speakers to avoid feedback.

(c) *Care of equipment*. A teacher must make pupils realise the importance of looking after expensive equipment, setting it up and putting it away properly at the end of a session.

(d) *Tempo*. A band may not realise that the reason their music is not 'breathing' is because they are taking it too fast or too slow. It is remarkable how much more fluent, say, an improvised lead-guitar solo becomes after the teacher has suggested and set a different tempo.

(e) *Transposition*. Bands usually learn new material from records. Often these are in impossible keys for inexperienced instrumentalists, and the vocal range unsuitable for the singers available. A teacher can help by showing how to transpose. I have seen reggae pianists become adept transposers out of sheer necessity. This is an example of a 'traditional' musicianly skill, which many conservatory students find hard to master, developing through a pop idiom.

(f) *Composition and arranging*. Pupils should be encouraged to originate material of their own, and a teacher can help with compositional techniques, especially those which involve planning a musical structure. Bands have often sought my advice on how to begin, how to end, and how to arrange the order of events in an extended piece. A band can be shown how to plan a well-shaped performance, at what point the lead guitarist should take over from the singer for a solo, and at what point the singer should return. Terms such as 'Intro', 'Coda', 'Verse', 'Middle eight' are worth teaching to pupils who play in bands, as they facilitate discussion.

It is important to leave a band to rehearse itself a great deal of the time. In no sense is the teacher's role here that of a choir-trainer or conductor. Pupils must learn, both musically and socially, to cope with working with each other. Different bands may show different levels of success at working together; some will be ill-disciplined and waste time, others will rehearse purposefully and methodically. A teacher can arrange performance opportunities: school assemblies, concerts, dances and, possibly most educational of all, recording sessions. I have taken bands to the ILEA recording studio, and the experience has proved salutary for some of the less disciplined bands. They have been made aware that every second of studio time counts, and, hearing a multi-channel playback of themselves for the first time, they have learnt to listen as never before.

During the first year at my last school, I obtained a drum kit, an electric guitar, a bass guitar, an amplifier and a speaker. I later added an electric organ, a public address system with microphones, and another amplifier and speaker. It was then possible for singers and instrumentalists to sing and play together using this equipment. There is no doubt that there is a demand to make this kind of music, which attracts pupils with a wide range of backgrounds and abilities. Reggae is certainly an activity in the spirit of comprehensive education. In the same band one may find a remedial pupil playing alongside an A level student.

I was fortunate to have specialist teachers for keyboard, guitar, bass guitar and drums. These instruments were taught in groups of three or four pupils at a time. Between lessons, pianists and guitarists will practise on their own, but I have noticed that bass and drums prefer to practise together, forming the nucleus of a rhythm section. After a time, bass and drums may be joined by piano and melodica, making simple improvisations ('jamming') over repetitive riffs. It is from such beginnings that a band will develop.

Although at first bands will want to copy performances heard on records, I have been keen to encourage creative work in composing and arranging. A excellent piece of work by a particularly talented group of boys was an arrangement of Gershwin's 'Summertime'. This evolved over a period of several months. First, the bass guitarist conceived an ingenious reggae bass line, and over this three members of the group, the lead singer, the guitarist and the pianist worked out and sang a three-part vocal harmonisation. The working-out of the vocals was done away from the electric instruments, using only piano or acoustic guitar as accompaniment. In the final version, the first verse was sung in 'close harmony', and the second as a solo by the lead singer with sustained chords hummed by the other two. A number of other textures were explored with great ingenuity by these boys, whose singing went well into the male alto range. After a session of this vocal composing, which would often last well over an hour after school, they always appeared elated, having continually sparked ideas from one another. Indeed, I think they got more pleasure from these afternoons of working together, getting to grips with the material of music, than they got out of performing in public to an appreciative audience of their peers.

Providing resources and time for bands to rehearse has revealed talents which would have otherwise lain dormant. It has helped socialise pupils whose attitude was one of alienation, by giving them an activity which gives a sense of purpose and achievement. Understandably, the membership of reggae bands is almost entirely West Indian, although white pupils do play and sing in one or two of the bands. Reggae also tends to be a male province where instrumentalists are concerned. However, there are one or two good girl keyboard players and drummers, and our most inventive songwriter was a girl.

All this development takes time. It cannot be hurried along. During the past years there were frustrating times when I felt we weren't achieving very much. The

patterns shown in Example 2; these may be clapped separately or together. A more complex pattern is given in Example 3, in which only one complete pattern is shown.

Example 2

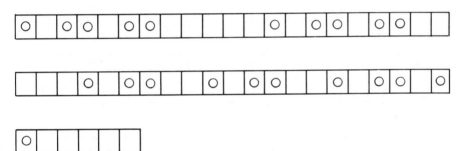

Example 3

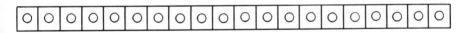

Some basic patterns

Example 4 shows the basic beat which is clapped or tapped by one pupil. Examples 5, 6 and 7 are all rhythms which can be tapped against pattern 4. They should first be taught separately, then taught with Example 4, and then combined (see Example 8), so that the relationships between the four patterns can be appreciated.

Example 4

Example 5

Example 6

O	O		O	O		O	O		O	O		O	O	

Example 7

O	O	O		O	O	O		O	O	O		O	O	O		O	O	O	

Example 8 (Examples 4–7 combined)

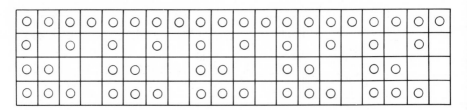

Once such patterns have been mastered, further, more complex rhythms can be introduced and the children themselves may be able to suggest suitable ones. Example 9 might emerge in this way for instance.

Example 9

In African music the basic pattern is usually played on the gong-gong. The main function of the gong-gong is to keep a steady time for all the drummers. This does not mean that the gong-gong only plays beats which are equidistant; it often plays a pattern which is interesting in its own right as well as being a reference point for all the other parts. All other players relate their own rhythms to that of the gong-gong, thus creating a complex overall pattern in which the different drum rhythms may not be directly related to each other. Part of the fascination of the music is to come to an understanding of these interrelationships. In traditional drumming the gong-gong rhythm does not usually give a steady pulse, but for teaching purposes it is preferable to start by doing so.

All the examples given so far are characteristic of African social drumming, i.e. drumming which arises at social occasions such as parties, and which accompanies general dancing. Example 10 shows the gong-gong rhythm which would normally provide the basic beat for other patterns on such occasions.

Example 10

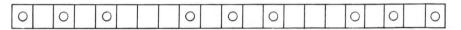

As in most African music, it does not fall on or state a 'basic beat' of the type which we would expect to find in a piece of Western music. Though the gong-gong provides a reference point for the performers and dancers, from a European point of view the parts are 'out of phase' with each other, in the way illustrated in Example 1. To make this point absolutely clear, in Example 11, Examples 5, 6 and 9 have been given together with Example 10. Note that Examples 5, 6 and 9 thus start 'one box later' than when they were given independently of the gong-gong rhythm of Example 10.

Example 11 (Examples 5,6,9,10 combined)

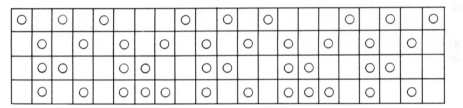

Further rhythms will be given later, but, in order to make them more authentic, they should be related to specific instruments. A description of some of these instruments now follows.

The drums and how they are played

I shall not attempt to describe all the drums typically used in West African music, but have instead selected a few and have described the role they play on particular traditional or ceremonial occasions.

THE KPANLOGO DRUM

This is a drum commonly used by the Ga people of Ghana. It is played with the hands as shown in Fig. 1. It is used for social drumming, i.e. whenever groups of people are gathered together for social occasions as opposed to official or traditional ceremonies. The drummer can display his virtuosity by inventing interesting and rapid rhythms to contrast with the supporting drums.

Fig. 1 Kpanlogo drum   *Fig. 2 Atsimevu*

THE ATSIMEVU

The Atsimevu is the master drum used by the Ewe people of Ghana. This drum used to be carved from a whole tree trunk but now the villagers have developed the art of coopering. As shown in Fig. 2, the master drummer stands to play this drum. He hits the drum with two sticks, or one hand and one stick. He can also produce a further sound by hitting the side of the drum with the stick.

The range of tones available to the drummer is wider for the Atsimevu than for any of the other drums. Its role is usually that of a master drum in the dance called Atsiagbekor. The master drummer issues complex phrases which direct the dancers in precise movements. There are over two hundred different signals, which the master drummer plays against a background of supporting drums playing fixed parts.

THE DONNO DRUM

The most popular and widely used drum in Africa in the double-headed Donno drum. It is used for both social and traditional drumming. The Donno frame is hollowed out of one piece of wood and has a head on each end. As can be seen in Fig. 3, it is played by being held under the arm and struck with a curved stick. The drum-

Example 12

Example 13 shows two Donno rhythms. An upper and lower note are shown for each drum, produced by squeezing the drum as previously described.

Example 13 (Donno drum)

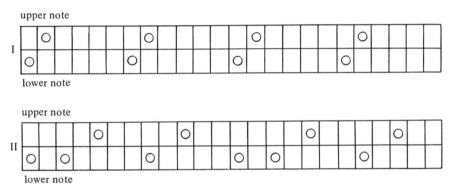

Examples 14, 15, 16 show three rhythms suitable for playing on frame drums.

Example 14

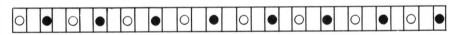

Example 15

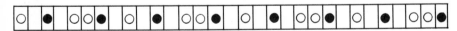

Example 16

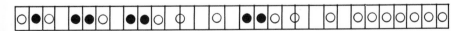

The frame drums are the most suitable for adaption to classroom use, since they are the simplest to reproduce if authentic drums are not available. All three rhythms shown in Examples 14–16 can be played together:

Example 17
(Examples 14, 15 and 16 combined)

There are many more rhythms which can be played on frame drums and as the basic patterns become more familiar it becomes easier to create individual patterns.

In the basic Gome rhythm shown in Example 18 the muted notes are played by placing the heel on the skin near the ground while the hands play at the top of the skin. Thus the muting here is achieved by a method not used in any of the other drums.

Example 18 (Gome drum)

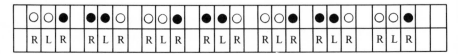

The gong-gong is struck with a stick. In notating it the upper and lower notes have been shown at higher and lower levels respectively. Example 19 is the Atsiagbekor rhythm.

Example 19 (gong-gong)

upper note

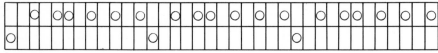

lower note

The upper note in Example 20 represents the shaker being hit against the palm of the left hand, held flat above the shaker. The lower note represents the shaker hit against the thigh, while seated.

Example 20 (shaker)

upper note
(palm)

lower note
(thigh)

Singing accompanied by playing

Much African music incorporates singing. (An example of Ewe singing with drums can be heard on the record *Ewe music of Ghana*, recorded and edited by S. K. Ladzekpo in the ASCH series, AHM 4222. The Mustapha Tettey Addy record given under 'Further resources' also includes some singing.)

Although it would be very difficult to teach songs in an African language without the guidance of a native speaker, it may be interesting and useful to give two examples of songs in the Ga language, set against a typical African rhythm (unfortunately the tune is not given). The songs are set out as follows:

GS: song in standard Ga orthography
AP: approximate pronunciation, using English spelling
ET: English translation

Song 1
GS: Mele ni yaa ee damɔʃi maʃɛ bo
AP: Mayle niyaa ay damoshe me shebo
ET: *Tell the ship that is going, to wait for a message*
                                            (twice)
GS: Kɛ otee yaa kɛ mantsɛ Taki akɛɛ miŋbi lɛee
AP: Ke otay yaake manche Taki ake mingbi lay
ET: *If you go, send my greetings to King Taki*
GS: Kɛ nigbɛ wɔ yaa, wɔ yaa Adabrakaa wɔamɔ gbɛee
AP: Ke nigbe woyaa woyaa Adabraka wuamo gbayee
ET: *I'm going to Adabraka to reserve a place*

Song 2
GS: Nyɔŋ tsele ni edʒee wɔ baa ʃwee wɔ baa gboo
AP: Nyong chele ni edje worbaa shwear worbaa gboo
ET: *Here is the new moon. We are going to play until we drop.*
                                            (twice)

As Example 21 shows, it is very possible and enjoyable to accompany well-known songs in English with the same beat. Ideally the drums used should be those indicated, but whatever drums are available can be used to good effect.

Creative drumming

Once the children have started playing the drums and have learned some traditional African rhythms, it becomes possible for them to attempt some free social drumming, that is, drumming improvised on a basic beat, using African rhythms. I give below one or two approaches which have proved successful in class in stimulating children to invent their own rhythms.

Example 21

(* 3 beats in the time of 4 boxes for the gong)

Gong
Frame
Kpanlogo
Shaker

1.	Me	le	ni	yaa	ee			da	mɔ	ʃi	ma	ʃɛ	bo	
	Me	le	ni	yaa	ee			da	mɔ	ʃi	ma	ʃɛ	bo	kɛ
	o	tee	yaa	kɛ	man	tsɛ	Tak	i a	kɛɛ		miŋ	bi	lɛee	kɛ
	nig	bɛ	wɔ	yaa,	wɔ	yaa	Ada	bra	kaa		wɔa	mɔ	gbɛ	ee	kɛ
	nig	bɛ	wɔ	yaa,	wɔ	yaa	Ada	bra	kaa		wɔa	mɔ	gbɛ	ee	
2.	Nyɔŋ	tse	le	ni	ed	zee	wɔ	baa	ʃwɛɛ		wɔ	baa	gboo		"	"
	"	"	"	"	"	"	"	"	"	"	"	"	"	"	"	"
3.	Baa		baa		black		sheep		Have you	any		wool?	
	Yes		Sir,		yes		Sir,		Three	bags		full.		etc.
4.	Jingle		bells,		Jingle		bells,		Jingle	all	the	way.		etc.
5.	Three		blind		mice,				Three	blind		mice.		etc.

(1)   The children may be asked to imitate the noise of galloping horses. They do this orally, and are then asked to clap the rhythm or tap it on the desk top. Finally they are asked to interpret it on a drum. Different groups may not come up with the same pattern, but usually the basic one which emerges is that given in Example 22 (a). Other groups in the class can then add their own patterns, and the whole is played against the basic beat given by the gong (or gong substitute).

Example 22

(* 3 beats in the time of 4 boxes for the gong)

Gong
(a)
(b)
(c)

orate explanations of the moods, colours and emotions associated with certain melodic structures. These ideas were developed between the fifth and eleventh centuries. One landmark was the division of the scale into twenty-two quarter tones (*srutis*), in contrast to the twelve European semitones; this is one factor which gives Indian music its distinct and unusual sound.

MEDIEVAL

In this period numerous writers invented new melodies, time systems and other techniques which added to the raga system. Perhaps the greatest musical commentary was written in the thirteenth century by Sarangadeva who classified ragas according to the seasons and times of the day, accompanied by elaborate descriptions of how to play each raga. The laws respecting the seasons, moods and times of performing ragas are still observed by modern Indian musicians. The association of mood, emotion and imagery with each raga, which is unique to Indian music, provided the basis for superb pictorial representations of ragas in the famous *Ragamala* paintings.

The Islamic invasion in the eleventh century had begun a cultural renaissance in India. Several musicians were inspired to create new styles. The legendary Amir Khusru developed a Muslim/Hindu singing style called *Khyal* which later became known as the *Qawali* style of singing. The heroic princess Mirabai abandoned worldly comforts and travelled barefooted, singing songs to Lord Krishna. Many of her songs have been recorded by well-known artists. It is interesting to know that most musicians were poets and philosophers who played and sang their own compositions. Since there was nothing comparable to Western notation in India, the individual styles and compositions were transmitted orally from father to son or guru to disciple in the utmost secrecy. Some modern musicians can trace their style of music right back to this Early Moghul era.

MODERN

During the British period music became much more confined to the courts where musicians had been employed by the leading princes for centuries. The British were generally uninterested in Indian music, with the exception of a few scholars such as Sir William Jones, Sir W. Ousley and Captain W. A. Willard. Indian authors continued to write about the music. Among them was the great poet Rabindranath Tagore, who also composed music. One of his songs 'Janagana' is the national anthem of India. When the radio and cinema were introduced in the thirties, the music which had previously been confined to the royal courts became available to the masses. Musicians experienced an economic freedom that opened up new horizons within and outside India. In the late fifties and early sixties, Indian music began to influence Western artists as varied as the Beatles, Traffic, Indo-Jazz Fusions, John McLaughlin, the Rolling Stones, Stockhausen, Quintessence, Theodorakis and John Cage. An LP recording was made by Yehudi Menuhin and Ali Akbar in the sixties and since then other cross-cultural links have followed in Britain and America.

This interest by Western musicians, combined with the fact of the presence of immigrant pupils in many British schools, the aesthetic value of the music itself and the educational value of coming to know another culture are, I believe, strong arguments for finding a place in the music curriculum for an introduction to this ancient but still vital form of music.

An Indian performance

An interesting way to introduce Indian music is to discuss the basic difference between a Western and an Indian concert. For example, a Western concert will have an orchestra, conductor and sometimes soloists, who perform the works of a great composer. But an Indian concert has no orchestra, conductor or composer. There will only be a group of three or four musicians, seated crosslegged on a carpet, with a cluster of burning incense at their side to help set the mood. The lead soloist sings or plays the melody (*raga*) with a rhythm accompaniment (*tala*) played by the drummer and the third musician plays the *drone* (*tambura*). The audience participates by following the music closely and showing its appreciation of the musicians' artistry right through the performance. Most of the music is improvised and the individual musician explores the infinite possibilities of the music with his own creative, artistic and technical skills.

At first the music may sound strange and even monotonous to Westerners, but after a while, one begins to notice the exciting interplay between melody and rhythm. Indian classical music doesn't have 'melody', as conceived in the West. There are no simple successions of notes in short, clear-cut phrases, such as are found in much European folk music, for example. Instead, each piece has recurring themes which are elaborated by grace notes and melodic sequences. But such a tune is never repeated exactly. Most performances begin with the drone, followed by the lead soloist stating the notes and mood of the raga on the sitar, sarod, flute, shahnai or other melodic instrument. The music begins slowly, but gradually builds up speed as the tabla player (drummer) joins in. The music gets faster and more complicated as it progresses, until it accelerates into a dense and complex final section, ending in a great climax.

Creative projects

Understanding the rules of rhythm (*tala*) and melody (*raga*) are the first steps towards enjoying the music. The following projects are based on the *raga*, *tala* and *drone*, but they are not totally authentic since it is difficult to convey an accurate representation of Indian music through Western notation and instruments. I have tried to make things clearer by preceding each project with an explanation which may be worth conveying to the pupils before they begin. The following suggestions apply to all the projects.

Seating: pupils should be arranged in a semicircle with the teacher at one end, or right in front of group.

Numbers: smaller groups are preferable though not obligatory (or essential).
Instruments: obviously we cannot re-create the sound of Indian instruments such as
the sitar and tabla, but we can try to produce something similar, bearing in mind the
limitations of classroom instruments. Here are a few suggestions:

(a)   The *drone* sounds better if it is played on instruments that can sustain the
       notes or produce a fine resonance, e.g. cello, piano, bass glockenspiel, bass
       xylophone and appropriate orchestral instruments. Suitable effects can also be
       added on the guitar, especially if one uses a 'folk' or prepared tuning (for
       guidance on this, see pp. 22–3).

(b)   The *raga* melody can be played on most melodic instruments such as recorders,
       xylophone, chime bars, glockenspiels and violins.

(c)   The *tala* can be played on many rhythm instruments including bongos and
       hand drums of different sizes.

Duration: this will range according to individual circumstances.

THE DRONE

The best way of coming to recognise, enjoy and appreciate the use of a drone is to
listen to a short, simple Western piece (e.g. some Bach organ pieces, bagpipe music,
pentatonic folk song) and to hum the tonic note at the same time. From this, the
listener will come to realise the harmonic function of the drone notes. The main difference between the drone in bagpipe music (or any European music) and in Indian
music is that the Indian drone notes are not played simultaneously like a chord, but
as single notes articulated in sequence. The Indian drone instrument or *tambura* has
four long strings which are usually tuned to the tonic octave and the note a fourth
or fifth above the tonic. The *tambura* has a 'twangy' sound which makes the notes
overlap into each other, creating a somewhat hypnotic effect.

Project 1 – Drones

Stage 1. The children work out the drones of scales and tunes (e.g. A minor; short
       bagpipe or recorder tunes).

Stage 2. The teacher plays or sings each scale or tune, the children droning with a
       definite rhythm for about 4–8 bars. The children then attempt the scale or tune
       while the teacher sustains the drone.

*N.B. The drone always starts, playing for about two bars before the tune or scale
comes in, and then continues to the end.*

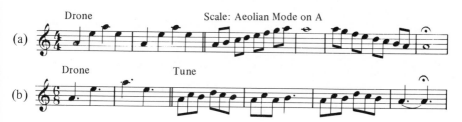

Stage 3. The class is divided into 2 groups.

Group a. plays/sings the drone.

Group b. plays/sings the scale or tune.

Stage 4. Groups change instruments and playing/singing parts.

Stage 5. The children can choose their own tunes and play drones to them. *Also* they can play the same tunes with traditional Western drones (first and fifth as a *chord*), being asked to notice the difference.

Work on drones can be developed by making links and comparisons with the relevant projects outlined by Paynter and Aston (1970). Some pupils may also be able to make links with the many rock pieces which do not use drones, but which do emphasise a repeated tonic note.

RAGA (MELODIC COMPOSITION)

The term *raga* has various definitions, one of which is this quotation from an old Indian text:

A raga, the sages say, is a particular arrangement of sounds in which notes and melodic movements appear like ornaments to enchant the mind.

(Sangita-drapana)

It has also been translated as an *'air'*, *'tune'* and often as a *'melody'*, but perhaps the nearest equivalent in Western terms is really *'a melodic composition'*. Each raga is considered to be endowed with aesthetic and spiritual qualities. It has its own mood and expression and is meant to have a distinct psychological and emotional effect on the listener and can therefore be related to colour, and visual image. This approach to music may be unfamiliar to some modern music lovers in the West, but in fact for the greater part of musical history the power that music has over the emotions has been an acknowledged universal mystery. Even in relatively recent times it is noteworthy that, in the West, the composer Scriabin gave colours to the notes of the scale.

In Indian music, each raga is believed to possess unique characteristics and is played according to its mood and the time of day or season with which it is connected. For example there are morning, evening and midnight ragas. There are also ragas that are played during the hot and rainy seasons though the rules guiding performance are not absolutely rigid. Just as a Western musician would not play an exciting waltz at a funeral, in the same way an Indian musician has to be sensitive to the time and mood of the raga.

Each raga must have at least five notes and it can be distinguished from other ragas in a number of ways:

(1)   The ascending and descending scale (which can vary).

(2)   Two main notes called *vadi* and *samvadi* (or 'king' and 'chief minister' notes) which are like poles around which the melody revolves. It is important to remember that Indian musicians never strike the tonic or main notes conspicuously. Instead they slide from side to side around them with the help of

grace notes (and other ornamentation) and then come to rest on the chief notes.

(3) The recurring melodic phrases special to the raga.

(4) The mood which pervades the whole performance like a spell.

All the complex devices of Indian music including grace notes, quarter tones (*srutis*), scale patterns, melodic phrases and other embellishments help to accentuate the mood of the raga. These are of course refinements which it is not possible to introduce in the elementary stages of study described in this article.

Project 2 – Raga moods and their scales

In this kind of work it is worth having a tape recorder which provides the chance for pupils to hear their own playing.

Stage 1. Play a few of the ragas in Example 1 in their ascending and decending forms on the piano. Accompany the ragas by playing the drones in the bass; hold down the sustain pedal so as to get a greater resonance and continuity of sound. It may be helpful to play the ragas both out of tempo and in a definite rhythm so that the pupils can see how the basic interval pattern of the raga can come to take on a definite 'melodic' shape.

The ragas given in Example 1 are mostly pentatonic and have the *same* ascending and descending pattern.

Stage 2. Give the children the opportunity to explain and discuss their personal feelings about each raga, e.g. whether it expresses joy, sorrow, excitement and so on.

Stage 3. Group pupils into pairs, ask each pair to choose a raga and to practise the drone and the scale.

(In the first instance it may be helpful or necessary for the teacher to adopt   me some sequence such as the following:

lead pupils in playing the scale in some simple rhythm pattern, e.g. four crotchets to crotchets to a bar of $\frac{4}{4}$ time;

ask the pupils to do the same without the teacher;

ask pupils to find a new rhythm pattern.)

Stage 4. Each pair plays its raga, exploring more freely (one pupil has the drone and the other the scale pattern).

Stage 5. Pupils swap parts and instruments.

If desired, each pair can then present its raga to the whole class.

N.B. The drone always starts, playing for about two bars before the scale or tune comes in, and then continues to the end.

Example 1

(a) RAGA REWA Time: late morning

Mood: tender and loving
Scale or Tune

(b) RAGA DHANI Time: late morning   Mood: happy and poetic

(c) RAGA MADHYAMADI SARANGA Time: midday   Mood: brilliant and confident

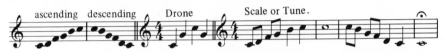

(d) RAGA MALAKOSHA Time: midnight
Mood: peaceful and sublime

Drone: B E

Project 3 - A raga tune and drone

Here is a short tune based on *raga Vibhasa* which is played at sunrise and expresses loveliness, enchantment and beauty.

Example 2

(a) RAGA VIBHASA Time: dawn
Mood: loveliness of early dawn

(b) Tune

Stage 1. Note that the markings *t(tonic)*, *v(vadi)* and *s(samvadi)* show how the melody is centred around the *v* and *s* notes.

Stage 2. Pupils can be divided into two groups, one playing the tune and the other the drone.

Stage 3. The children can be invited to improvise a tune which is based on the same plan (*vadi* and *samvadi*).

The ease with which pupils are able to produce ideas which are creative and yet adhere to the underlying principles will depend greatly on their natural aptitudes and their previous experience of creative musical work. When difficulty is experienced, it may be helpful to lead the pupils into autonomous creative work by the following procedures:

(i)   by the use of a call and response technique, i.e:

the teacher leads – the pupils imitate

the pupils lead – the teacher responds, giving a model of a creative response

the teacher leads – the pupils give a creative response

the pupils take on both roles

(ii)   the teacher shows how the call and response can be linked into one longer phrase, played by one person

(iii)   the results can be recorded for playback and comment either in the same lesson or at the next meeting. This can avoid the complications of using notation, which for many pupils can be inaccurate, tedious, time-consuming and discouraging.

TALA (RHYTHM CYCLE)

In Western music, the tempo of a piece may slow down or speed up for dramatic emphasis, but in an Indian piece there is only one tala or rhythm cycle right through. In some respects there is a parallel to tala in much blues music which repeats itself in a twelve-bar cycle. However, unlike the blues, in which ornamentation and variation takes place *over* a basic metre and harmonic structure, an Indian piece will develop intricate patterns and subtle divisions *within* the basic tala (especially as the music progresses towards the end of a performance).

The *tabla* provides the rhythmic accompaniment for most Indian music. The treble drum or *daya* (RH drum) is tuned to the tonic and the bass drum or *baya* (LH drum) plays the dominant. There are many rules governing the use of tala; here are some of the most basic ones.

(1)   Every tala must end on the principal notes of the raga (i.e. *vadi or samvadi*). This is called the *sam* beat and audiences often applaud (or show other signs of approval) when the soloist returns to the *sam* (rather as they do in jazz concerts when, after a spectacular flight of improvisation, a soloist 'lands' the first beat of a new cycle).

(2)   Each tala has a *sam* beat and a *khali* (or silent) beat; this pattern is clapped out in a special way. The *sam* is indicated by clapping on the beat, whereas the *khali* is shown by a wave of the hand.

(3)   The *khali* beat always comes just before the *sam* beat and the drummer has to

indicate this in his playing by missing out the bass drum on this beat. This provides an important guide for the soloist because, in a complex improvisation, the lighter weight of the *khali* beat is always there to lead him back home to the *sam.*

Drummers have to study and use a system of *mnemonic syllables* called *bhols* which tell him how the drum accompaniment should be beaten out. Many recordings have drummers saying these rhythmic syllables aloud.

Project 4 – Talas

The talas in Example 3 have their Indian syllables (*bhols*) written with them. Each tala can be either said or clapped. Alternatively they may be arranged (according to their sound) for various percussion instruments.

Example 3

(a) DADARA TALA   6 time units and 1 main beat

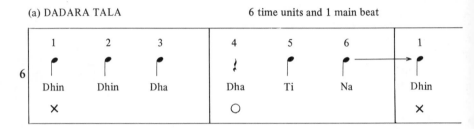

(b) RUPAKA TALA   7 time units and 3 main beats

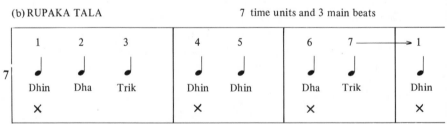

N.B. This tala does not have a silent beat

(c) JHAPA TALA   10 time units and 3 main beats

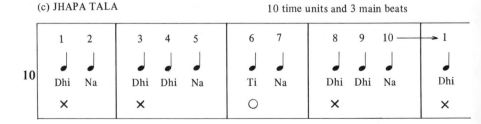

Co-operation is the key to Gamelan music. There are many different kinds of Gamelan, but most comprise metallophones of different sizes constructed on similar principles to the vibraphone, suspended gongs with a central boss, smaller ones mounted horizontally in racks, small cymbals and a pair of drums.

The average Gamelan has around fifteen to twenty players. Each member of the ensemble plays a part which may not be especially interesting or may even be meaningless on its own, yet when combined with the others produces a resultant interlocking pattern of great vitality and complexity, requiring a performance of the utmost rhythmic precision. As there is no conductor, the success of the ensemble depends on the art of listening to one another. The qualities required in the musicians are also recognised as crucial in Western music; it is for this among other reasons that I believe Balinese music to be relevant to the British classroom.

Rhythmic co-ordination

The following exercises and projects are designed to develop rhythmic sense. If an individual pattern is not performed with complete accuracy the whole ensemble will fail. This fact should enhance the individual's sense of involvement in a group. Experience shows that pupils are likely to pass quickly from a stage of seeing the music as 'exotic' to that of giving their attention to its fundamental 'abstract' values.

Let us start with a rhythmic exercise which leads gently into Balinese musical ideas by means of familiar Western patterns, using the first and most important musical instrument: the human body. If each pupil claps a relatively simple pattern (repeated) it can be made to interlock with others and produce a resultant stream of even notes. This is how Balinese music (not unlike medieval European hocketing) gets much of its characteristic energy and excitement. A very effective way of doing this to begin with is by rhythmic canon, using a pattern which everyone will know. One which certainly fulfils this condition and has the added benefit of a reasonable complexity and buoyancy is the following (originally suggested by Piers Spencer):

♩=120   (repeated ad lib.)

Ideally the group should stand in a circle, and each entry in the canon should start one crotchet beat after one complete rendition of the pattern (i.e. nine crotchets later). The resultant pattern will be a stream of quavers; classes are usually quite excited by the way this happens.

The Kecak chorus

The leap from the above type of exercise into Balinese music is not great. The famous Kecak (Ketjak) chorus, nowadays chanted (not sung) by more than a hundred men imitating the chattering of monkeys in dance dramas based on the Ramayana epic, is built on the same principle of interlocking patterns, though they are not necessarily canonic.

Example 1

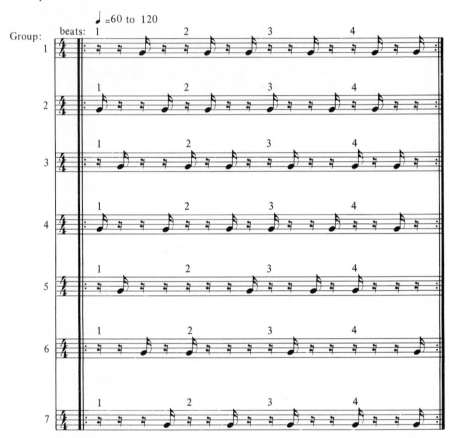

Example 1 is the kind of thing which makes up Kecak. Although patterns for seven groups are given, it will be seen that the continuous stream (in this case of semiquavers) can be achieved with just the first three groups (or by various other combinations). The full ensemble of seven groups is designed to thicken the sound and make the structures less symmetrical and obvious. Each pattern should be mastered before any other one is added to it.

Pupils are quite capable of moving on from given exercises such as this to the invention of interlocking patterns of their own. Such work can be profitably linked with other approaches to creative rhythmic activity, such as the game 'Plug' (Wishart, 1974), which sets out to develop a similar sense of rhythmic interplay.

The syllable used in the chant is 'chak' pronounced sharply and dryly with a glottal stop at the end rather than a distinct 'k', thus there are no pitches involved. It should be ensured that the sound of the syllable is right, or at least that the sounds of the whole class blend. It will probably help if some kind of pulse is kept, possibly a straight crotchet pulse on one note of a xylophone, and/or a little ostinato melody, perhaps the following:

Although Kecak chanting seems to go at great speed it will be found to be just as effective at quite a slow tempo, because the main thing is the complete regularity of the resultant stream. The tempo should be increased only when the patterns have been completely mastered. Apart from experiments with tempo, further variations may be obtained by changing the dynamics. The best way to do this is by a sudden change from one extreme to the other. For example, four bars of very loud chanting could be followed by four bars at a very low volume after a sharp drop at the beginning of the fifth bar.

Melodic applications

The Gamelan music of Bali uses the same principle of interlocking patterns, though the polyphony is, if anything, even denser and the music uses distinct pitches. Underpinning the structure is a melody moving slowly in even units of time, punctuated by the large gongs. It is above this melody that the smaller metallophones weave their complex embellishing patterns, the whole thing being directed by one or more drums. The relationship between slow melody and embellishing patterns is not arbitrary; in fact it suggests a musical game which is also excellent ear training. In the slower and more sedate Gamelan music of Central Java (the island to the West of Bali) it is actually possible to deduce the main melody from one of the embellishing patterns, as the following example should make clear:

This procedure can be adapted to our 'Balinese' music. First it is necessary to choose a scale. Assuming one is using Orff percussion (the obvious choice), it is wise to restrict the instruments to those notes. Balinese scales are mostly pentatonic. The most common one (arranged for Western instruments) is:

Another is:

Yet another is the familiar 'black-note' pentatonic scale which, though not widely used in Bali, is associated with the quartet of metallophones which accompany shadow plays:

Taking the first of these scales, one instrument or group could improvise or pre-compose a melody in even notes at a slow tempo and another two instruments or groups could play two interlocking patterns above it. The rhythm of these patterns should be worked out beforehand. The players should also decide which notes can go with particular melody notes. Such preparatory work can be undertaken without notation and memorised. This is an advantage in classes which have problems with reading music (it is in fact the authentic Balinese approach). From this point on, the music can become a game of 'follow-my-leader', with the embellishing groups improvising a response to a melody which they may be hearing for the first time! Let us examine how this response may be built up.

The embellishing patterns must include the melody note, and move closely around it. Thus something along the following lines could be agreed:

embellishing notes:

melody notes:

The rhythms of the two interlocking parts must also be worked out. Here is a typically Balinese version, which pupils could first clap until they have mastered and memorised it:

(repeat ad lib.)

The resultant melody of the two interlocking parts shows the sort of movement to be aimed at (see Example 5). In fact, the melody was worked out first and the individual interlocking parts were derived from it (which, as I have already mentioned, is a good way of ensuring the correct result).

Example 5

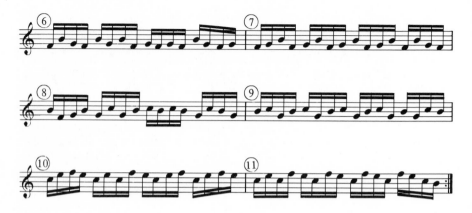

Conclusion

Throughout this chapter I have avoided anything which is a pure, unadulterated and finished Balinese product. Instead I have shown how simplified ideas from Balinese music may be used to create pieces and how all kinds of variations and experiments can be tried out. It can be argued that this is more in keeping with the Balinese spirit than presenting complete genuine pieces with instructions to perform them as they stand, since in Bali much of the music is worked out in rehearsal and any member of the Gamelan – and even anyone in the gathering of interested and involved spectators – is free to make suggestions and have them tried out and discussed. The Hindu Balinese are an intensely religious people and no less intensely creative. Music is not a sacrosanct collection of given, unalterable compositions. Rather it is a communal expression, the result of a corporate effort to produce something as good as possible to serve the occasion and please the audience of both gods and mortals.

Reference

Wishart, T., *Sounds Fun: A Book of Musical Games* (Schools Council Project, University of York, 1974).

Further resources

BOOKS

The great work on Balinese music in English is Colin McPhee's *Music in Bali* (Yale University Press, 1966) which contains many photographs and musical examples, some of which could be taken as the basis of further pieces, though they are, not surprisingly, more complex than the ideas in this chapter. Shorter accounts of Gamelan music are by Mantle Hood in *Music* (Handbuch der Orientalistik, Brill,

1972) and by William Malm in *Music Cultures of the Pacific, the Near East and Asia* (Prentice-Hall, 1977). Chapter 2 of Christopher Small's *Music–Society–Education* (John Calder, 1977) is a stimulating discussion of the role of music in Bali and Africa, while Jack Dobbs' article 'Music and children in Bali' (Music in Education, August 1978) considers the relevance of Balinese music in education both in Bali and England.

RECORDS

There are many records of Balinese music. General collections of non-Western music which include fine examples from Bali are the Nonesuch Explorer series, the *Unesco Collection – Musical Atlas* (EMI), the *Unesco Collection – Musical Sources* (Philips), and various LPs by Ocora records. The record entitled *Golden Rain* (Nonesuch Explorer series, H-72028) gives extended examples of the modern Balinese Gamelan and Kecak chorus.

The Information Department of the Indonesian Embassy, 38 Grosvenor Square, London W1, has a collection of slides, films and tapes, and the embassy also houses a beautiful Gamelan from Central Java (not Bali).

PART FOUR ALTERNATIVES

Editors' preface

We have devoted the final section of this book to the exciting work which has been done at the Central London Youth Project Music Workshop. It therefore falls into a very different category from the rest of the work described in this book for at least two reasons. Firstly, the teaching does not take place in a school, but at a youth club to which pupils from a number of London schools go. Secondly, the two tutors are not qualified *music* teachers, but are themselves experienced rock musicians. Therefore their manner of teaching is, not surprisingly, rather different from most of the projects described in earlier sections of this book, since these have been designed for the more traditional music teacher, who may not even have much knowledge of popular music.

We believe, however, that the experience of the Basement Youth Club provides useful lessons not only for other local education authorities who could set up similar centres to help service their secondary schools, but also by suggesting ways in which ordinary schools could profit from the experience of the teaching at the club.

Paul Crawford's chapter describes the origins of the project, its organisation and funding. It also contains numerous very helpful hints for teachers who are encouraging the growth of pupil rock bands in their schools. Again, there is useful, practical advice concerning such things as equipment, safety and security for those rare schools which have the possibility of turning part of a music wing into a rock music studio. The chapter also demonstrates the pedagogical benefits of being prepared to accept the musical tastes of pupils whatever they may be and the importance of the personal relationship between teacher and pupil. Nicholls' (1976) account of the music department at Countesthorpe College, a comprehensive school near Leicester, suggests that the distinctive nature of the teaching and learning at the club is not a totally impossible state for a school to aspire to.

Stewart Knight's chapter focusses on the more technical side of the teaching. The wealth of detail given dispels any myths concerning the idea that the intuitive and improvisatory nature of rock music means it cannot be taught. The graded programme of instruction for the guitar could act as a model for all teachers who wish to begin their guitar tuition using rock and blues, rather than classical or folk music. Of especial value is his description of the 'box system' of presenting rock scales and riff patterns. Since this system is being increasingly widely adopted by writers of popular music instruction manuals for guitar, the reader with only a classical guitar training (or none at all) is likely to find these comments a valuable first step towards the use of such books.

Stewart Knight's account also shows how this type of work may be matched with the requirement that music be taught to largish groups simultaneously. His (and other teachers') experience shows that it is certainly possible to teach guitar classes by a mixture of teacher exposition and mass participation, with valuable results. A useful extension of this approach is indicated in Chapter 6 by the comments of Felix Cross and Elspeth Compton who indicate types of activity which, though based upon the assumption of a common core of instruction in a given lesson, do permit pupils to participate simultaneously at varying levels of skill. For example, Elspeth's 'rhythm doodle' is an activity which presupposes little skill and imposes few limits; it could evoke both very elementary and very sophisticated responses from the same group.

The detailed suggestions which Stewart Knight gives about how to rehearse rock music groups should prove very useful to all those teachers engaged in such extra-curricular work in schools. However, he also states that he believes that such work can be undertaken only by those with appropriate (preferably professional) experience. His anxiety on this matter reflects the concern expressed in the latter part of Ed Lee's chapter on guitar teaching. On the other hand, his view conflicts with the assumption which underlies virtually all the other contributions, which is that goodwill, backed up with effort and study, will take the teacher a long way towards initiating work which is valuable in itself, and attracts many pupils who would otherwise reject school music.

Certainly, Stewart Knight's experience suggests that there are pupils with whom motivation and authenticity of idiom must always be the first consideration, even at the cost of setting aside some of the other aims of the teacher. The success of the Basement Project indicates to us that any aesthetic disadvantages are far outweighed by the fact that a large number of people, who would otherwise remain outside music, can come to have a highly motivated involvement in it, which in many cases also acts as a major factor in their personal development and acquisition of self-confidence.

It is not possible in this context fully to reconcile the various conflicting beliefs, but it is possible to note points on which all contributors would agree. First, specialist knowledge is undoubtedly required with more advanced pupils. Second, contact with the real world in which the large majority of professional musicians earn their living must surely be healthy in its effect. Third, the sheer bulk of popular music, its vast popularity and its intrinsic value suggest that in formulating a curriculum, specialist knowledge of the popular field should certainly be drawn upon, even if it is not deemed acceptable for such specialists to supervise all such work in a school. Finally (a point which we hope and believe does not need to be reiterated to our readers), every music teacher, of no matter what personal preference, needs to recognise the skill of the popular musician, and the degree of knowledge and intensity of study which thus underlies every stage of the work which Stewart Knight describes.

Reference

Nicholls, M., 'Running an "open" music department', in Vulliamy, G. and Lee, E. (eds.), *Pop Music in School* (Cambridge University Press, 1976; 2nd edn 1980).

14 The Central London Youth Project Music Workshop

PAUL CRAWFORD

Background

The CLYP is a small independent charitable organisation based in Covent Garden in London's West End. It runs a 'voluntary-aided' youth club in the 'Basement' which is funded in three ways: the ILEA provides two full-time workers, sessional payments for specialist activity tutors and contributes to running costs; the London Borough of Camden provides a director-administrator's salary for the CLYP and a substantial contribution to running costs; finally, private charities have given much support in capital equipment, the cost of building improvements and, for the first six months of its full-time activity, the salaries for the music workshop's two tutors, Stewart Knight and myself.

The Basement functions as a local youth club but also attracts, because of the musical activities, many young people from outside the immediate neighbourhood. The active membership is about equally drawn from each group. The club is open six nights a week (afternoons too, during school holidays) and a practice room fully equipped for rock group rehearsals is available for use during all of this time.

There are five evening sessions per week of guitar and electric bass lessons, shared amongst three tutors, and one session of drum lessons. Since September 1978 there have been eight half-day sessions per week with groups from London schools; these are organised as day-link courses to complement the schools' musical activities.

About four times a year there are performance evenings at the Basement (or in the summer, outdoors on the stage of the Covent Garden Community Festival); at these events the more established groups perform. An important element in the Music Workshop's programme is performances by other young bands at the Basement. We have had an average of one band a week for the last two years, thus giving the young groups a chance to play and the Basement members a chance to hear what other bands are doing.

There has been a youth club in the Basement since 1972, arising out of the campaign to save the area from the Covent Garden Plan. The community groups which coalesced to fight the proposals succeeded in preventing the demolition of many nineteenth-century industrial buildings; it is one of these warehouse basements which, after continued local pressure, was converted into a youth club. Music was introduced under the auspices of Anthony Hoskyns, a local schoolteacher, who provided some equipment and money.

Stewart and I became involved when the band of which we were then members played at the Basement. We were impressed by the space itself and the positive attitude of the then full-time youth worker in charge, David Lamont. We agreed to pay a return visit, and then went on to get other bands we knew to play. Gradually, we started to promote weekly 'gigs' using our own equipment and transport in return for the use of space to rehearse and play in. As we got to know the kids, the more interested ones naturally asked us to help them with their playing.

During the latter part of 1976 there occurred one of the periodic upheavals which voluntary groups seem to visit upon themselves. Out of this emerged CLYP. In fact, the youth club staff, membership and premises remained the same except for the loss of the two part-time music tutors introduced by Anthony Hoskyns. Consequently Stewart and I were asked to take over the responsibility for the whole music programme.

The CLYP is a limited liability company registered as a charity with the Charity Commissioners. This status has considerable advantages in both management and fund-raising. It gives independence in matters of policy and day-to-day administration to the Council of Management and the staff. This permits flexibility and cuts out red tape. Matters of policy are decided by the Council of Management (at present eight strong). The Council is composed of local parents, a former London Borough of Camden alderman with experience of youth work, and a local schoolteacher. In practice the staff attend most Council meetings and are consulted on matters of policy. The day-to-day running of the youth club and music workshop is delegated to the staff concerned who meet regularly and co-operate in matters of common concern such as performance events, discipline and supervision of the rehearsal room.

It is impossible to separate the social and musical activities of the club: it is a meeting place for young musicians as well as a place where they can learn, practise and perform. Hence the music tutors are youth workers, too, and the full-time youth workers help to supervise some musical activities. However, the budgets of the two operations are quite separate. There are established means of support for a youth club and this is secure; the Music Workshop, however, has to patch its finances together as best it can. The semi-independent status of CLYP is of some help here.

Private charitable trusts are more willing to give a substantial lump sum of money for non-recurring capital expenditure than to enter into an annual revenue commitment such as the employment of staff. The Music Workshop has constantly suffered, therefore, from the opposite problem to that of the schoolteacher: whereas in schools there are full-time staff but often very low budgets for equipment, the Basement has always managed to provide professional equipment for its students, except in the very early stages, when this was loaned by the tutors. On the other hand, securing permanent salaries for the two tutors has been a constant nightmare and is still unresolved.

In the early stages the work was voluntary but, as the workshop grew, further funding was sought. In this the ILEA Youth Service was very supportive and flexible. 'Club Classes' are sessions paid for specialist work; in practice they predominantly provide sports coaching. Throughout our time at the Basement the Tutor Warden for Camden and the North London Area Youth Office have supported the teaching work done and, wherever possible, provided specialist sessional fees for it. However, these tutor sessions are operative only during school term time (although available only through evening youth clubs) and each is only two hours long. Since Basement teaching continues throughout the year and each session is of four hours, less than half the work done has actually been paid for. Without these sessions, though, the teaching would never have become established, and they still provide a valuable means of introducing new part-time teaching staff who become available. In June 1978 a 75 per cent salary for two tutors was grant-aided by a trust for six months. When that expired at the end of November, the CLYP ran into deficit, as a promised further grant failed to materialise. At the time of writing these problems remain unresolved, though there has been a temporary alleviation of some difficulties thanks to an emergency grant from the ILEA.

The conclusions to be drawn from these unhappy experiences are clear for all to see. The Music Workshop, like any other educational structure, cannot produce good quality work and develop without full-time salaried staff. It is neither good practice nor reasonable to rely on goodwill alone. There is a limit to what can be expected of youth (or other public service) workers, many of whom now feel in their more pessimistic moments that their attitude is one not of determination, but of a mere obstinate refusal to face the fact of society's indifference and hypocrisy towards the very grave problems which face young people in the inner cities. Words and fine sentiments are not enough: if there are to be worthwhile schemes to help the young (of which we believe the Music Workshop to be one) society must back its concern with cash.

Nature of the space

The Basement is in the centre of London's music business. It is five minutes' walk from the Marquee, the Rock Garden, Charing Cross Road (where all the music shops are) and round the corner from the old punk rock club the Roxy. There's no doubt this gives it a certain cachet for people who come and learn there. Furthermore it looks like one's idea of a rock club – the opening scenes of *Quadrophenia* were filmed there. It's an attractive and atmospheric venue, important qualities in any artistic venture.

More practically, its walls are four feet thick and it's completely underground in the basement of a five-storey warehouse, so sound proofing is not much of a problem. The importance of this can't be over-stressed: it's quite impossible to run a rock venue in unsuitable premises, since if there's sustained opposition from the neighbours, you're bound to be forced out. And rock music *is* loud: much of its

few minutes with a bass guitar and a 100 watt amplifier going through it. The Basement's equipment is as follows:

1 HH VS Musician combo (amp and speakers in one unit) 100 W
1 HH IC100 combo, 100 W
1 Vox AC30 combo (nominally 30 W but pretty loud)
1 Selmer 50 W bass amp coupled to a reflex-ported bass enclosure containing
    2 RCF L15P100A 15 in loudspeakers, each with a 4 in edge-wound voice coil
    and metal dust cap, which is good for projecting higher partials.
1 Hayman drum kit with 4 drums including metal shell snare drum, plus hi-hat,
    crash and ride cymbals.

This equipment is kept in the practice room and used, when necessary, on stage for performances. The instruments available, though not kept permanently in the practice room for security reasons, are as follows:

2 Sakura 'Strat-type' 6-string electric guitars
2 Sakura 'Les Paul-type' 6-string electric guitars
1 Shaftesbury 'Telecaster-type' bass guitar
1 Crumar electric piano
1 Takamine 6-string flat-top acoustic guitar (steel string)

Often musicians will bring their own instruments, but this number of guitars is required to run rehearsals and lessons simultaneously. The above equipment represents an outlay of nearly £2000. It has all survived two years of very intensive use and is highly recommended. There is also a large amount of ancillary equipment: leads, straps, stands, mikes, etc., and it is this which requires most maintenance. The soldering iron is needed most days for some minor repairs.

We are ruthless about security. The equipment is attractive, valuable and marketable. When not in use the instruments are kept in a locked cabinet in a locked room. The practice room has a Chubb mortice lock. The Basement itself has only two doors, both steel-plated and with Chubb mortice and padlocks. Fortress-like security is essential. If there were any windows they would have bars on them. If the club were a soft touch it would get broken into. We have made it harder to 'do' than the West End music shops nearby on the theory that people will be less tempted to steal from us than from them. All the equipment is insured, of course. As a consequence, we have not had a major item stolen since we started. We are very firm that anybody found taking anything, however unimportant, is banned permanently. Everyone understands this policy and knows that it will be enforced. On the couple of occasions that something of this type has disappeared and the culprit has not been discovered, we have closed the Music Workshop for a fortnight, suspending all lessons and rehearsals. One of the items concerned was a blown chassis loudspeaker worth nothing. It is a matter of professionalism not to leave anything exposed to risk; to know who is using any piece of equipment at a given time; to make them know they're responsible for it; to check it after use; and to show anger if anything goes missing or is wilfully damaged. In the latter case we give people the choice of paying for it or never coming back.

There is a 50p per hour nominal charge for the practice room which is payable on booking it. This is charged mainly to stop people booking it frivolously or wasting time in it. Equipment is never lent for outside events unless it's in the care of a member of staff, and then as rarely as possible. Most wear and tear and most risk of theft is to equipment in transit. The intensity with which the equipment is used in the workshop is enough to justify its cost without letting it go out. Most of the equipment is used on most days and we couldn't manage without it in the event of some mishap.

The practice room is our most intensively used facility. It is used in the daytime for link-course sessions and in the evening for (mainly) unsupervised rehearsals by club members. It is booked so heavily that each group is rationed to one two-hour session per week. The room is not booked more than a fortnight ahead in order to prevent the exclusion of some groups because of extensive advance booking by others. Everything runs smoothly because the room has good equipment with no set-up time for the musicians, and because the sound insulation and security mean that there is no trouble to anyone else. We are planning a second practice room in an adjacent basement; this will no doubt be booked out solidly too. There is no question that many school buildings are unusable for this kind of activity and no amount of goodwill (or expenditure) will overcome the inherent deficiencies in sound insulation and security from which they suffer. This is a prime reason for our popularity with local schools.

PERFORMANCE

Live performance is an important test of musicianship. It is essential in order to provide a focus for all the other activities of the music workshop and a deadline against which to work. Only those ready for such exposure are asked to play: it can be shattering to someone's confidence to make them perform too soon. But there's nothing to match the intensity and excitement of performance, and much about communication with other musicians and an audience can only be learnt on stage. Nothing helps a young musician's confidence and self-assurance like a successful performance; and nothing punctures the pretensions of a 'poser' like a disastrous one. The Basement fills a need by giving many aspiring young groups a chance to perform. Apart from occasional end-of-term concerts at school, outlets for them are very scarce. Most semi-pro groups work in pubs, graduating to the better-known ones on the music circuit and eventually to the well-known rock venues in Central London. To do this needs a lot of equipment and resources of transport, publicity and management. Few young groups can afford all these to start off with. A non-commercial venue like the Basement provides a stepping stone and helps avoid having to jump straight into the commercial music scene prematurely.

The Basement's equipment is of a professional standard and gives young groups a chance to learn in professional surroundings with a real audience. The PA system comprises:

1 12-channel in, 2 out MM PA mixer (MP 175)
2 HH 100 W 'slave' amplifiers
2 Vector 2 X 15 in speaker reflex-port bass enclosures fitted with 15 in Goodman Audiomax speakers
2 Vector HF projectors, each fitted with 1 RCF TW101 100 W compression driver on a short horn behind a slant-plate acoustic lens with integral passive crossover.
Assorted mikes and stands

It is essential to have an operator who understands sound equipment to help the band get a decent sound and take care of any emergencies that may arise during the performance. The Basement PA does not have vocal monitors, so the vocalist finds it hard to hear what he or she is singing. We hope to remedy this soon – a fold-back outlet is provided on the mixer to drive monitors and we occasionally use a spare HH combo for this purpose, but it's far from ideal.

A variety of fairly cheap (under £50) tuning machines are now on the market. We have a 'Diotuner' (manufactured by A. M. Marshall, 3 Doughty St, London WC1, 01-405 9966 and distributed mainly by Rose-Morris) and it is vital for en-suring good performances. Making sure one's tuning is accurate is difficult at the best of times since tuning to equal temperament by ear is not an elementary task. Many performances by both young and experienced groups have foundered either when individual tunings have diverged during a set or because of inordinate delays between numbers while this was eliminated. A tuning machine has the advantage of being silent and swift.

Many of the young bands who play at the Basement are not regulars and we are able to advise them about equipment, transport, management, union and legal prob-lems, publicity, relations with the press, record companies, promoters, agencies, making demo tapes and innumerable details of running a band of which they have limited experience. We can also act as an informal booking agency, recommending the best of them to local promoters.

Our most successful performance evenings have, nonetheless, been those which involved 'in-house' groups both from school day-link courses and evening Music Workshop members, when friends and relations of the groups have come to see what they have achieved. Apart from being enjoyable and friendly occasions, they show what a combination of dedicated commitment, technique, thorough prepara-tion and good equipment can achieve: they have been *musically* successsful, with-out any allowance having to be made for the musicians' youth and relative inex-perience. After such an evening we always have a surge of applications to join the Music Workshop from other young people who are keen to emulate the success of the existing groups.

Conclusion

The CLYP Music Workshop is a forum for young musicians to meet and progress. The equipment and expertise is available for them to improve their playing to the limit of their talent and commitment. Music is a major interest of young people, a means of self-expression that is creative, non-competitive yet still demanding (and rewarding) the highest standards of skill and excellence. Young people come from as far afield as Bow, Hammersmith, Walthamstow and Streatham to practise regularly at the Basement. There are hardly any other opportunities in London for young people to practise loud electric music with good equipment in suitable surroundings. Yet CLYP is not able to publicise its facilities because it is already stretched to the limit. The enthusiasm with which the ILEA (through its music inspectorate and many school heads of music) has supported the project is a testimony to how difficult it is to provide this facility in schools and yet how much it is in demand. It's as though there were in London only one football pitch or one swimming pool. We therefore hope that we can extend our facilities, but we hope most of all that our experience will encourage others to start similar schemes.

have heard on records. Consequently, before we teach them any chords at all, we ask them what sort of music they like, and which song in particular they would like to learn. If a pupil chooses a song which, on the record, has a chord sequence of

$$\frac{4}{4} \| \quad \text{Bm} \quad | \quad \text{F}\sharp \quad | \quad \text{A} \quad | \quad \text{E} \quad | \quad \text{G} \quad | \quad \text{D} \quad | \quad \text{Em} \quad | \quad \text{F}\sharp 7 \quad \|$$

('Hotel California' – The Eagles)

and that pupil has never played a chord before, then it is clear that by transposing it down a tone, the chords Bm, F♯ and F♯7, which would undoubtedly cause the pupil considerable difficulty at this stage, can be eliminated. The transposed sequence

$$\frac{4}{4} \| \quad \text{Am} \quad | \quad \text{E} \quad | \quad \text{G} \quad | \quad \text{D} \quad | \quad \text{F} \quad | \quad \text{C} \quad | \quad \text{Dm} \quad | \quad \text{E7} \quad \|$$

will be much easier for the pupil to play – the chord which is most likely to prove a stumbling block being the F major chord, which could be simplified as a chord played on the top three strings, or the top four strings, depending on the pupil's ability.

Having worked through this sequence by learning the chords first individually, then in pairs, then in two groups of four bars, then joining the two four-bar sequences together, and finally concentrating on any particularly difficult chord changes, the pupil has not only learnt how to play eight different chords, he also has a very strong motivation to practise them in the form of an eight-bar exercise which he himself suggested. Another song is then dealt with in the same way. If this second song contains no new chords, the teacher can transpose it into a key which will involve the introduction of some new chords, once again simplifying these if necessary to avoid fingerings which the pupil would find too difficult at this stage (e.g. C9 could be replaced by C7, or even C major).

We show the pupil how these chords can be shown as chord diagrams, e.g. G7 can be represented as

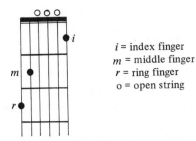

i = index finger
m = middle finger
r = ring finger
o = open string

One reference sheet which we frequently use is a sheet containing eight blank chord windows on which a chord sequence containing up to eight chords can be drawn. There is another sheet with sixteen blank windows for longer sequences. A third sheet is also given to pupils, showing the chord diagrams for about twenty common chords.

Topic ID, dealing with picking and strumming techniques, is covered at the same time as the left-hand positions are learnt. As soon as the pupil has mastered about 15–20 simple chords, and can play them smoothly in the songs of his choice, he moves on to the first section of work concerned with single-line playing. We draw his attention to the 'one finger per fret rule', which teaches him that when he is playing in the VIIth position, say, any note played at the seventh fret must be played with the index finger, any note at the eighth fret, with the middle finger, and any note at the ninth and tenth frets must be played with the ring and little fingers, respectively. He then applies this to the scale of C major played at the VIIth position, involving the use of all four fingers of the left hand, and also useful as an exercise in co-ordinating the left and right hands.

Full six-string major and minor barré chords and their alterations to form dominant seventh and minor seventh barré chords are covered next. These chords are practised by substituting them for the simple chords in the songs which the pupil has already learnt, and/or by learning how to play new songs containing these four types of barré chord. If at this stage, or indeed when chords are first encountered, the pupil fails to suggest a suitable song, the teacher can consult the index of songs (item (e) in the list of materials) in order to find a suitable exercise for the pupil (e.g. for barré chords, two songs listed in the song index are 'Here, There and Everywhere' by the Beatles, and 'Interstellar Overdrive' by the Pink Floyd).

The final topic in Stage I is concerned with single-line playing once again, but this time not with the major diatonic scale, but with the minor pentatonic blues scale. This scale is formed from the first, flattened third, fourth, fifth and flattened seventh degrees of the major scale. This scale is an important basic element of rock music, and is particularly common in improvised guitar solos (where the major scale is very rarely used). First the pupil learns how to play a two-octave blues scale, as follows:

In conjunction with this, we show the pupil the basic conventions of the guitar tablature system which we use. This system can be used with ordinary five-line stave manuscript paper, and is more convenient than other forms of tablature which are based on a six-line stave.

Essentially, the four spaces in the five-line stave are used to represent the inside four strings of the guitar, B, G, D and A, from top to bottom. The space above the top line represents the top E string, and the space below the bottom line, the bottom E string. Where a string is played fretted, this is indicated by the fret number written in the appropriate space; an open string is indicated by an O in the appropriate space. Conventional symbols for note duration are written below the stave. So the blues scale described above would be written in guitar tablature thus:

As well as being easy to read and write, this form of notation is preferable for much of our work since it is a more economic way of writing out guitar parts, and it also facilitates the very accurate notation of certain techniques which conventional staff notation has no simple way of expressing clearly. The most important of these techniques are introduced at this stage, notably string bending, releasing a string, the 'hammer-on', the 'pull-off', slide vibrato.

For example, raising the pitch of a fretted note, by either pushing or pulling the string, and releasing the string back to the original note can be indicated in tablature thus:

where P indicates that the third string is pushed, from the tenth fret, where it is originally played, up to the note which can be obtained two frets higher (12), and then released (R) back to the original note.

Having learnt these techniques, the pupil is then given a reference sheet of practice phrases, or 'runs', using the blues scale, for which there is an accompanying cassette (both items prepared by the tutors) which the pupil can work with at home.

In Stage II the pupil will encounter more fingering patterns (or 'boxes') for the blues scale, and in accordance with the overall scheme of instruction in this topic, the two-octave blues scale described at the end of Stage I is referred to as 'Box A' (in the key of C) (see Fig. 1).

The introduction of the pupil to this system is very important for various reasons. Firstly, it is rapidly becoming standard in the rock field. It was devised in America, and is a feature of most of the best tutor books from the USA, and notably the series produced by Green Note (see Resources). Secondly, the system begins to lead the pupil away from the rote learning of individual phrases towards the conception of a pervasive scale structure out of which rock ideas are generated.

During the course of these first 15–20 lessons, the pupil will have asked the tutor to teach him how to play various songs, and in view of the constant release of new records, some of these will be unfamiliar to the tutor. In these cases the pupil is asked to bring a copy of the record to his lesson; the tutor records it on a cassette and transcribes whatever the pupil wants for the next lesson. The tutor comes to this lesson with the cassette recording of the song and a copy of the transcription

Systems of notation

(Blues scale – key C – notes C_E♭_F_G_B♭_C Position VIII)

(1) Box notation (Box A)

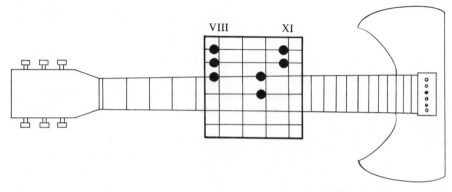

This diagram represents a small section of the finger board– from fret VIII to fret XI. Normally the picture of the guitar is not given; it is included here for greater clarity.

(2) Comparison of standard notation and guitar tablature.

Note the difference between this (six-line) tablature, which is that found in most tutor books, and our own (four-space) tablature, described earlier.

Fig. 1

(the original copy being filed for possible future reference). We use published sheet music only very occasionally, since (a) the songs are frequently not available in published form, and (b) when they are, the published music is often not very reliable. The teacher then works through the song with the pupil, piece by piece. Since it is often necessary to go over the same very short section of music several times, a cassette machine with cue and review facilities, which enable this operation to be done quickly and simply, is virtually essential. In fact a very robust and efficient cassette player is a vital teaching aid. It is sometimes necessary from the point of view of

one or more members of the group. If the group decides to 'cover' a song already recorded by other artists, the teacher records it on a cassette (unless he knows it already, and can teach all the group members their parts straight away). The tutor prepares for the session by transcribing the song for the group, simplifying any parts that are too difficult. Each section of the song is then learnt individually, e.g. introduction, then verse, then chorus etc.

In order to minimise the amount of time wasted by other players while one pupil is shown his part, the teacher must use his discretion in the way he teaches the group how to play the song. If all the parts are fairly easy, he can show each person in turn what to do, and get them to practise quietly while he moves round the group. He needs constantly to draw the pupils' attention to guitars which have gone out of tune and so are spoiling what would otherwise be a good performance. The band then practises the particular section being dealt with until it is good enough for them to be taught the next section. When this has been mastered, the group then practises joining these two sections together. Subsequent sections are added on one by one in the same way, until the complete song is ready to be rehearsed. Re-listening to the original recording is useful in setting a standard for the band to match. The finishing touches are then added to the song, e.g. introduction and ending, dynamics and solos.

In some cases, especially in more complicated songs, it is important to write the song on a board (basically in the form of a chord chart) and ask the pupils to copy it and file it away. Keeping a file of songs is useful for future reference, even though much of the music is played by ear at the time. Songs which groups at the Basement have learnt in this way include 'One Nation Under a Groove' by Funkadelic, 'Jamming' by Bob Marley, 'Hey Joe' by Jimi Hendrix, and 'Do Dat' by Grover Washington Jr.

Rehearsing an original song puts an even greater emphasis on group discussion, co-operation and constructive criticism, and the teacher's roles here include mediator and critic, as well as provider of musical ideas which might contribute to the song. It is important to find the right balance between completely prepared music and the inclusion of passages which give the players freedom to contribute a creative element. All rehearsed songs which the group regard as completed should be recorded in rehearsal – even if only on a cassette machine – for critical appraisal by the group.

In group sessions, the kind of instruction given to the bass player, drummer and keyboard player varies with the competence of each pupil and with the type of music being played. A pupil playing the drums for the first time is introduced to the names of each part of his kit, and we give him a demonstration of how the various drums and cymbals are used in the sort of music which his group wants to play. For example, for a rock band playing rock-and-roll-derived music, we show the drummer how to play his bass drum on the beats 1 and 3, and his snare drum on beats 2 and 4. When he has co-ordinated these two things, we show him how to add his closed hi-hat or ride cymbal, played in quavers, eight to the bar, giving the complete drum part as shown below.

Cymbal
Snare drum
Bass drum

The addition of the cymbal to the bass and snare drums often takes some time to master. Then we show pupils who have achieved this how to use the tom-toms to produce rolls, which help to punctuate the music, and also how to use the crash cymbal and bass drum to emphasise certain points in the music. When teaching a reggae group, it is useful to show the drummer how to produce the 'clave' sound from his snare drum by resting the tip of the left stick on the upper head of the drum and bringing the stick down on to the rim of the drum. We also stress the importance of the drummer and the bass player playing together as a unit.

In the case of the bass guitar, the first thing which we normally ask the beginner to do is to play the root note of each chord in the song which his group are playing. When this has been mastered, we often then show him how to add other notes (usually the third and the fifth) to make the part more interesting. In reggae songs, the bass part normally consists of several riffs, repeated throughout the song. It is possible with most beginners to show them these riffs (which often contain the root and the fifth of the chord only) one at a time as the song is worked through. This is a typical riff:

chords: C   G

We show piano players who are new to the instrument how the keyboard is laid out as a repeated sequence of twelve-note 'blocks' (from C to B). Initially we ask them to play simple triads following the chord sequence of the song. In some cases the key-board plays a melody, which we show the pupil, and which he usually memorises from the demonstration. Written music is used very rarely, except by more experi-enced players. We sometimes write down the chords of a section of a song on pre-pared duplicated sheets, showing a section of the keyboard (about two octaves). A two-chord sequence can be written on this sheet by putting the symbol 1 on each note of the first chord, and 2 on each note of the second chord. In this way the pupil can tell by looking at the diagram of the keyboard where he should put his fingers on the piano.

We discuss many other points in these group sessions, e.g. the value of jamming occasionally to stimulate new ideas; how to plan a 'set' for a performance; the prob-lems connected with performing on stage which are not encountered in rehearsal, such as keeping all elements of the performance under control, particularly the volume and the tuning of the instruments; the importance of audience communication, and of doing a 'soundcheck' before starting; the care, maintenance and protection of of the instruments and a basic understanding of the equipment's construction and operation; and information about recording (if possible the group should do a recording session in a properly equipped studio).

It should be clear from the above why I feel that the effective supervision of a rock-group teaching session can be done only by someone who, as well as being an experienced teacher of pupils of a wide range of academic ability and motivation, also has a broad knowledge of many aspects of the music, and specific skills in the instruments played, as well as experience of making music in this type of group. Only such a teacher will be able most fully to capitalise on the considerable and expanding knowledge which the pupils themselves bring to the work.

Further resources

BOOKS

Mel Bay Publications Inc., *The Johnny Smith Approach to Guitar* (1971), Parts 1 and 2.
Pass, Joe and Thrasher, Bill, *Joe Pass Guitar Style* (Gwyn Publishing Co., 1970).
Roth, Arlen, *Nashville Guitar* (Oak Publications, 1977).
Snyder, Jerry (ed.), *Blues Guitar – A Method by B. B. King* (Charles Hansen Educational Music and Books, 1973).
White, Leon, *Styles for the Studio*, Vol. 1 (Dale Zdenek Publications, 1976).

Green Note Publications have issued a series of book/record sets over the past few years including *Improvising Rock Guitar* (1973) and volumes on electric blues, slide guitar, country rock and Nashville style.

PERIODICALS

Guitar magazine (published monthly by Musical New Services Ltd).
Guitar Player magazine (published monthly by GPI Publications).

RECORDS

Jeff Beck, *Wired*, Epic EPC 86012
Captain Beefheart and his Magic Band, *Trout Mask Replica*, Straight STS 1053
Chuck Berry, *Golden Decade*, Chess 6641 018
Butterfield Blues Band, *East–West*, Elektra EKS 7315
Chick Corea's Return to Forever, *Hymn of the 7th Galaxy*, Polydor 2310 283
Miles David, *Get Up With It*, CBS 88092
Buddy Guy, *Hold That Plane*, Vanguard VSD 79323
Jimi Hendrix, *The Cry of Love*, Track 2408 101
Howlin' Wolf (Chester Burnet), *Howlin' Wolf*, Chess 2CH 60016
Isley Brothers, *3+3*, Epic EPC 65740
B. B. King, *Live at the Regal*, ABC Paramount ABCS 509

John Mayall with Eric Clapton, *Blues Breakers*, Decca SKL 4804
Quicksilver Messenger Service, *Happy Trails*, EMI EST 120
Spirit, *The Twelve Dreams of Dr. Sardonicus*, Epic 64191
Muddy Waters, Chess *Blues Masters* Series, Chess 2ACMB 203
The Who, *My Generation*, Brunswick LAT 8616
Frank Zappa/Captain Beefheart/Mothers of Invention, *Bongo Fury*, Warner Bros
    DS 2234

Index

This is not an exhaustive index. The headings chosen are those that are particularly important or that have received more than passing reference in the text.